# This planner belongs to:

_______________

# 2026

## January

| S | M | T | W | T | F | S |
|---|---|---|---|---|---|---|
|   |   |   |   | 1 | 2 | 3 |
| 4 | 5 | 6 | 7 | 8 | 9 | 10 |
| 11 | 12 | 13 | 14 | 15 | 16 | 17 |
| 18 | 19 | 20 | 21 | 22 | 23 | 24 |
| 25 | 26 | 27 | 28 | 29 | 30 | 31 |

## February

| S | M | T | W | T | F | S |
|---|---|---|---|---|---|---|
| 1 | 2 | 3 | 4 | 5 | 6 | 7 |
| 8 | 9 | 10 | 11 | 12 | 13 | 14 |
| 15 | 16 | 17 | 18 | 19 | 20 | 21 |
| 22 | 23 | 24 | 25 | 26 | 27 | 28 |

## March

| S | M | T | W | T | F | S |
|---|---|---|---|---|---|---|
| 1 | 2 | 3 | 4 | 5 | 6 | 7 |
| 8 | 9 | 10 | 11 | 12 | 13 | 14 |
| 15 | 16 | 17 | 18 | 19 | 20 | 21 |
| 22 | 23 | 24 | 25 | 26 | 27 | 28 |
| 29 | 30 | 31 |   |   |   |   |

## April

| S | M | T | W | T | F | S |
|---|---|---|---|---|---|---|
|   |   |   | 1 | 2 | 3 | 4 |
| 5 | 6 | 7 | 8 | 9 | 10 | 11 |
| 12 | 13 | 14 | 15 | 16 | 17 | 18 |
| 19 | 20 | 21 | 22 | 23 | 24 | 25 |
| 26 | 27 | 28 | 29 | 30 |   |   |

## May

| S | M | T | W | T | F | S |
|---|---|---|---|---|---|---|
|   |   |   |   |   | 1 | 2 |
| 3 | 4 | 5 | 6 | 7 | 8 | 9 |
| 10 | 11 | 12 | 13 | 14 | 15 | 16 |
| 17 | 18 | 19 | 20 | 21 | 22 | 23 |
| 24 | 25 | 26 | 27 | 28 | 29 | 30 |
| 31 |   |   |   |   |   |   |

## June

| S | M | T | W | T | F | S |
|---|---|---|---|---|---|---|
|   | 1 | 2 | 3 | 4 | 5 | 6 |
| 7 | 8 | 9 | 10 | 11 | 12 | 13 |
| 14 | 15 | 16 | 17 | 18 | 19 | 20 |
| 21 | 22 | 23 | 24 | 25 | 26 | 27 |
| 28 | 29 | 30 |   |   |   |   |

## July

| S | M | T | W | T | F | S |
|---|---|---|---|---|---|---|
|   |   |   | 1 | 2 | 3 | 4 |
| 5 | 6 | 7 | 8 | 9 | 10 | 11 |
| 12 | 13 | 14 | 15 | 16 | 17 | 18 |
| 19 | 20 | 21 | 22 | 23 | 24 | 25 |
| 26 | 27 | 28 | 29 | 30 | 31 |   |

## August

| S | M | T | W | T | F | S |
|---|---|---|---|---|---|---|
|   |   |   |   |   |   | 1 |
| 2 | 3 | 4 | 5 | 6 | 7 | 8 |
| 9 | 10 | 11 | 12 | 13 | 14 | 15 |
| 16 | 17 | 18 | 19 | 20 | 21 | 22 |
| 23 | 24 | 25 | 26 | 27 | 28 | 29 |
| 30 | 31 |   |   |   |   |   |

## September

| S | M | T | W | T | F | S |
|---|---|---|---|---|---|---|
|   |   | 1 | 2 | 3 | 4 | 5 |
| 6 | 7 | 8 | 9 | 10 | 11 | 12 |
| 13 | 14 | 15 | 16 | 17 | 18 | 19 |
| 20 | 21 | 22 | 23 | 24 | 25 | 26 |
| 27 | 28 | 29 | 30 |   |   |   |

## October

| S | M | T | W | T | F | S |
|---|---|---|---|---|---|---|
|   |   |   |   | 1 | 2 | 3 |
| 4 | 5 | 6 | 7 | 8 | 9 | 10 |
| 11 | 12 | 13 | 14 | 15 | 16 | 17 |
| 18 | 19 | 20 | 21 | 22 | 23 | 24 |
| 25 | 26 | 27 | 28 | 29 | 30 | 31 |

## November

| S | M | T | W | T | F | S |
|---|---|---|---|---|---|---|
| 1 | 2 | 3 | 4 | 5 | 6 | 7 |
| 8 | 9 | 10 | 11 | 12 | 13 | 14 |
| 15 | 16 | 17 | 18 | 19 | 20 | 21 |
| 22 | 23 | 24 | 25 | 26 | 27 | 28 |
| 29 | 30 |   |   |   |   |   |

## December

| S | M | T | W | T | F | S |
|---|---|---|---|---|---|---|
|   |   | 1 | 2 | 3 | 4 | 5 |
| 6 | 7 | 8 | 9 | 10 | 11 | 12 |
| 13 | 14 | 15 | 16 | 17 | 18 | 19 |
| 20 | 21 | 22 | 23 | 24 | 25 | 26 |
| 27 | 28 | 29 | 30 | 31 |   |   |

# Year in Pixels

|     | J | F | M | A | M | J | J | A | S | O | N | D |
|-----|---|---|---|---|---|---|---|---|---|---|---|---|
| 1.  |   |   |   |   |   |   |   |   |   |   |   |   |
| 2.  |   |   |   |   |   |   |   |   |   |   |   |   |
| 3.  |   |   |   |   |   |   |   |   |   |   |   |   |
| 4.  |   |   |   |   |   |   |   |   |   |   |   |   |
| 5.  |   |   |   |   |   |   |   |   |   |   |   |   |
| 6.  |   |   |   |   |   |   |   |   |   |   |   |   |
| 7.  |   |   |   |   |   |   |   |   |   |   |   |   |
| 8.  |   |   |   |   |   |   |   |   |   |   |   |   |
| 9.  |   |   |   |   |   |   |   |   |   |   |   |   |
| 10. |   |   |   |   |   |   |   |   |   |   |   |   |
| 11. |   |   |   |   |   |   |   |   |   |   |   |   |
| 12. |   |   |   |   |   |   |   |   |   |   |   |   |
| 13. |   |   |   |   |   |   |   |   |   |   |   |   |
| 14. |   |   |   |   |   |   |   |   |   |   |   |   |
| 15. |   |   |   |   |   |   |   |   |   |   |   |   |
| 16. |   |   |   |   |   |   |   |   |   |   |   |   |
| 17. |   |   |   |   |   |   |   |   |   |   |   |   |
| 18. |   |   |   |   |   |   |   |   |   |   |   |   |
| 19. |   |   |   |   |   |   |   |   |   |   |   |   |
| 20. |   |   |   |   |   |   |   |   |   |   |   |   |
| 21. |   |   |   |   |   |   |   |   |   |   |   |   |
| 22. |   |   |   |   |   |   |   |   |   |   |   |   |
| 23. |   |   |   |   |   |   |   |   |   |   |   |   |
| 24. |   |   |   |   |   |   |   |   |   |   |   |   |
| 25. |   |   |   |   |   |   |   |   |   |   |   |   |
| 26. |   |   |   |   |   |   |   |   |   |   |   |   |
| 27. |   |   |   |   |   |   |   |   |   |   |   |   |
| 28. |   |   |   |   |   |   |   |   |   |   |   |   |
| 29. |   |   |   |   |   |   |   |   |   |   |   |   |
| 30. |   |   |   |   |   |   |   |   |   |   |   |   |
| 31. |   |   |   |   |   |   |   |   |   |   |   |   |

## Color Codes

## Notes

# January 2026

| MONDAY | TUESDAY | WEDNESDAY | THURSDAY |
|---|---|---|---|
|  |  |  | 1 |
| 5 | 6 | 7 | 8 |
| 12 | 13 | 14 | 15 |
| 19 | 20 | 21 | 22 |
| 26 | 27 | 28 | 29 |

# January 2026

| FRIDAY | SATURDAY | SUNDAY | NOTES |
|---|---|---|---|
| 2 | 3 | 4 | ○ |
|  |  |  | ○ |
|  |  |  | ○ |
|  |  |  | ○ |
|  |  |  | ○ |
| 9 | 10 | 11 | ○ |
|  |  |  | ○ |
|  |  |  | ○ |
|  |  |  | ○ |
|  |  |  | ○ |
| 16 | 17 | 18 | ○ |
|  |  |  | ○ |
|  |  |  | ○ |
|  |  |  | ○ |
|  |  |  | ○ |
| 23 | 24 | 25 | ○ |
|  |  |  | ○ |
|  |  |  | ○ |
|  |  |  | ○ |
|  |  |  | ○ |
| 30 | 31 |  | NOTES |

# February 2026

| MONDAY | TUESDAY | WEDNESDAY | THURSDAY |
| --- | --- | --- | --- |
|  |  |  |  |
| 2 | 3 | 4 | 5 |
| 9 | 10 | 11 | 12 |
| 16 | 17 | 18 | 19 |
| 23 | 24 | 25 | 26 |

# February 2026

| FRIDAY | SATURDAY | SUNDAY | NOTES |
|---|---|---|---|
|  |  | 1 | ○ |
|  |  |  | ○ |
|  |  |  | ○ |
|  |  |  | ○ |
|  |  |  | ○ |
| 6 | 7 | 8 | ○ |
|  |  |  | ○ |
|  |  |  | ○ |
|  |  |  | ○ |
| 13 | 14 | 15 | ○ |
|  |  |  | ○ |
|  |  |  | ○ |
|  |  |  | ○ |
|  |  |  | ○ |
| 20 | 21 | 22 | ○ |
|  |  |  | ○ |
|  |  |  | ○ |
|  |  |  | ○ |
|  |  |  | ○ |
| 27 | 28 |  | NOTES |

# March 2026

| MONDAY | TUESDAY | WEDNESDAY | THURSDAY |
|---|---|---|---|
|  |  |  |  |
| 2 | 3 | 4 | 5 |
| 9 | 10 | 11 | 12 |
| 16 | 17 | 18 | 19 |
| 23 | 24 | 25 | 26 |

# March 2026

| FRIDAY | SATURDAY | SUNDAY | NOTES |
|---|---|---|---|
|  |  | 1 | ○ |
|  |  |  | ○ |
|  |  |  | ○ |
| 6 | 7 | 8 | ○ |
|  |  |  | ○ |
|  |  |  | ○ |
| 13 | 14 | 15 | ○ |
|  |  |  | ○ |
|  |  |  | ○ |
| 20 | 21 | 22 | ○ |
|  |  |  | ○ |
|  |  |  | ○ |
| 27 | 28 | 29 | 30 |
|  |  |  | 31 |

| MONDAY | TUESDAY | WEDNESDAY | THURSDAY |
|---|---|---|---|
|  |  | 1 | 2 |
| 6 | 7 | 8 | 9 |
| 13 | 14 | 15 | 16 |
| 20 | 21 | 22 | 23 |
| 27 | 28 | 29 | 30 |

| FRIDAY | SATURDAY | SUNDAY | NOTES |
|---|---|---|---|
| 3 | 4 | 5 | ○ |
| | | | ○ |
| | | | ○ |
| | | | ○ |
| | | | ○ |
| 10 | 11 | 12 | ○ |
| | | | ○ |
| | | | ○ |
| | | | ○ |
| 17 | 18 | 19 | ○ |
| | | | ○ |
| | | | ○ |
| | | | ○ |
| | | | ○ |
| 24 | 25 | 26 | ○ |
| | | | ○ |
| | | | ○ |
| | | | ○ |
| | | | ○ |
| | | | NOTES |

# May 2026

| MONDAY | TUESDAY | WEDNESDAY | THURSDAY |
| --- | --- | --- | --- |
|  |  |  |  |
| 4 | 5 | 6 | 7 |
| 11 | 12 | 13 | 14 |
| 18 | 19 | 20 | 21 |
| 25 | 26 | 27 | 28 |

# May 2026

| FRIDAY | SATURDAY | SUNDAY | NOTES |
| --- | --- | --- | --- |
| 1 | 2 | 3 | ○ |
|  |  |  | ○ |
|  |  |  | ○ |
|  |  |  | ○ |
|  |  |  | ○ |
| 8 | 9 | 10 | ○ |
|  |  |  | ○ |
|  |  |  | ○ |
|  |  |  | ○ |
| 15 | 16 | 17 | ○ |
|  |  |  | ○ |
|  |  |  | ○ |
|  |  |  | ○ |
|  |  |  | ○ |
| 22 | 23 | 24 | ○ |
|  |  |  | ○ |
|  |  |  | ○ |
|  |  |  | ○ |
|  |  |  | ○ |
| 29 | 30 | 31 | Notes |

# June 2026

| MONDAY | TUESDAY | WEDNESDAY | THURSDAY |
| --- | --- | --- | --- |
| 1 | 2 | 3 | 4 |
| 8 | 9 | 10 | 11 |
| 15 | 16 | 17 | 18 |
| 22 | 23 | 24 | 25 |
| 29 | 30 | | |

# June 2026

| FRIDAY | SATURDAY | SUNDAY | NOTES |
|---|---|---|---|
| 5 | 6 | 7 | ○ |
|  |  |  | ○ |
|  |  |  | ○ |
|  |  |  | ○ |
|  |  |  | ○ |
| 12 | 13 | 14 | ○ |
|  |  |  | ○ |
|  |  |  | ○ |
|  |  |  | ○ |
| 19 | 20 | 21 | ○ |
|  |  |  | ○ |
|  |  |  | ○ |
|  |  |  | ○ |
|  |  |  | ○ |
| 26 | 27 | 28 | ○ |
|  |  |  | ○ |
|  |  |  | ○ |
|  |  |  | ○ |
|  |  |  | ○ |
|  |  |  | Notes |

# July 2026

| MONDAY | TUESDAY | WEDNESDAY | THURSDAY |
| --- | --- | --- | --- |
|  |  | 1 | 2 |
| 6 | 7 | 8 | 9 |
| 13 | 14 | 15 | 16 |
| 20 | 21 | 22 | 23 |
| 27 | 28 | 29 | 30 |

# July 2026

| FRIDAY | SATURDAY | SUNDAY | NOTES |
|---|---|---|---|
| 3 | 4 | 5 | ○ |
| | | | ○ |
| | | | ○ |
| | | | ○ |
| | | | ○ |
| 10 | 11 | 12 | ○ |
| | | | ○ |
| | | | ○ |
| | | | ○ |
| 17 | 18 | 19 | ○ |
| | | | ○ |
| | | | ○ |
| | | | ○ |
| | | | ○ |
| 24 | 25 | 26 | ○ |
| | | | ○ |
| | | | ○ |
| | | | ○ |
| | | | ○ |
| 31 | | | NOTES |

# August 2026

| MONDAY | TUESDAY | WEDNESDAY | THURSDAY |
| --- | --- | --- | --- |
|  |  |  |  |
| 3 | 4 | 5 | 6 |
| 10 | 11 | 12 | 13 |
| 17 | 18 | 19 | 20 |
| 24 | 25 | 26 | 27 |

# August 2026

| FRIDAY | SATURDAY | SUNDAY | NOTES |
|---|---|---|---|
|  | 1 | 2 | ○ |
|  |  |  | ○ |
|  |  |  | ○ |
|  |  |  | ○ |
|  |  |  | ○ |
| 7 | 8 | 9 | ○ |
|  |  |  | ○ |
|  |  |  | ○ |
|  |  |  | ○ |
| 14 | 15 | 16 | ○ |
|  |  |  | ○ |
|  |  |  | ○ |
|  |  |  | ○ |
|  |  |  | ○ |
| 21 | 22 | 23 | ○ |
|  |  |  | ○ |
|  |  |  | ○ |
|  |  |  | ○ |
|  |  |  | ○ |
| 28 | 29 | 30 | 31 |

# September 2026

| MONDAY | TUESDAY | WEDNESDAY | THURSDAY |
|---|---|---|---|
|  | 1 | 2 | 3 |
| 7 | 8 | 9 | 10 |
| 14 | 15 | 16 | 17 |
| 21 | 22 | 23 | 24 |
| 28 | 29 | 30 |  |

# September 2026

| FRIDAY | SATURDAY | SUNDAY | NOTES |
|---|---|---|---|
| 4 | 5 | 6 | ○ |
| | | | ○ |
| | | | ○ |
| | | | ○ |
| | | | ○ |
| 11 | 12 | 13 | ○ |
| | | | ○ |
| | | | ○ |
| | | | ○ |
| 18 | 19 | 20 | ○ |
| | | | ○ |
| | | | ○ |
| | | | ○ |
| | | | ○ |
| 25 | 26 | 27 | ○ |
| | | | ○ |
| | | | ○ |
| | | | ○ |
| | | | ○ |
| | | | NOTES |

# October 2026

| MONDAY | TUESDAY | WEDNESDAY | THURSDAY |
|---|---|---|---|
|  |  |  | 1 |
| 5 | 6 | 7 | 8 |
| 12 | 13 | 14 | 15 |
| 19 | 20 | 21 | 22 |
| 26 | 27 | 28 | 29 |

# October 2026

| FRIDAY | SATURDAY | SUNDAY | NOTES |
|---|---|---|---|
| 2 | 3 | 4 | ○ |
|  |  |  | ○ |
|  |  |  | ○ |
|  |  |  | ○ |
|  |  |  | ○ |
| 9 | 10 | 11 | ○ |
|  |  |  | ○ |
|  |  |  | ○ |
|  |  |  | ○ |
| 16 | 17 | 18 | ○ |
|  |  |  | ○ |
|  |  |  | ○ |
|  |  |  | ○ |
|  |  |  | ○ |
| 23 | 24 | 25 | ○ |
|  |  |  | ○ |
|  |  |  | ○ |
|  |  |  | ○ |
|  |  |  | ○ |
| 30 | 31 |  | NOTES |

# November 2026

| MONDAY | TUESDAY | WEDNESDAY | THURSDAY |
| --- | --- | --- | --- |
|  |  |  |  |
| 2 | 3 | 4 | 5 |
| 9 | 10 | 11 | 12 |
| 16 | 17 | 18 | 19 |
| 23 | 24 | 25 | 26 |

# November 2026

| FRIDAY | SATURDAY | SUNDAY | NOTES |
|---|---|---|---|
|  |  | 1 | ○ |
|  |  |  | ○ |
|  |  |  | ○ |
|  |  |  | ○ |
|  |  |  | ○ |
| 6 | 7 | 8 | ○ |
|  |  |  | ○ |
|  |  |  | ○ |
|  |  |  | ○ |
| 13 | 14 | 15 | ○ |
|  |  |  | ○ |
|  |  |  | ○ |
|  |  |  | ○ |
|  |  |  | ○ |
| 20 | 21 | 22 | ○ |
|  |  |  | ○ |
|  |  |  | ○ |
|  |  |  | ○ |
|  |  |  | ○ |
| 27 | 28 | 29 | 30 |

# December 2026

| MONDAY | TUESDAY | WEDNESDAY | THURSDAY |
| --- | --- | --- | --- |
|  | 1 | 2 | 3 |
| 7 | 8 | 9 | 10 |
| 14 | 15 | 16 | 17 |
| 21 | 22 | 23 | 24 |
| 28 | 29 | 30 | 31 |

# December 2026

| FRIDAY | SATURDAY | SUNDAY | NOTES |
|---|---|---|---|
| 4 | 5 | 6 | ○ |
| | | | ○ |
| | | | ○ |
| | | | ○ |
| | | | ○ |
| 11 | 12 | 13 | ○ |
| | | | ○ |
| | | | ○ |
| | | | ○ |
| 18 | 19 | 20 | ○ |
| | | | ○ |
| | | | ○ |
| | | | ○ |
| | | | ○ |
| 25 | 26 | 27 | ○ |
| | | | ○ |
| | | | ○ |
| | | | ○ |
| | | | ○ |
| | | | NOTES |

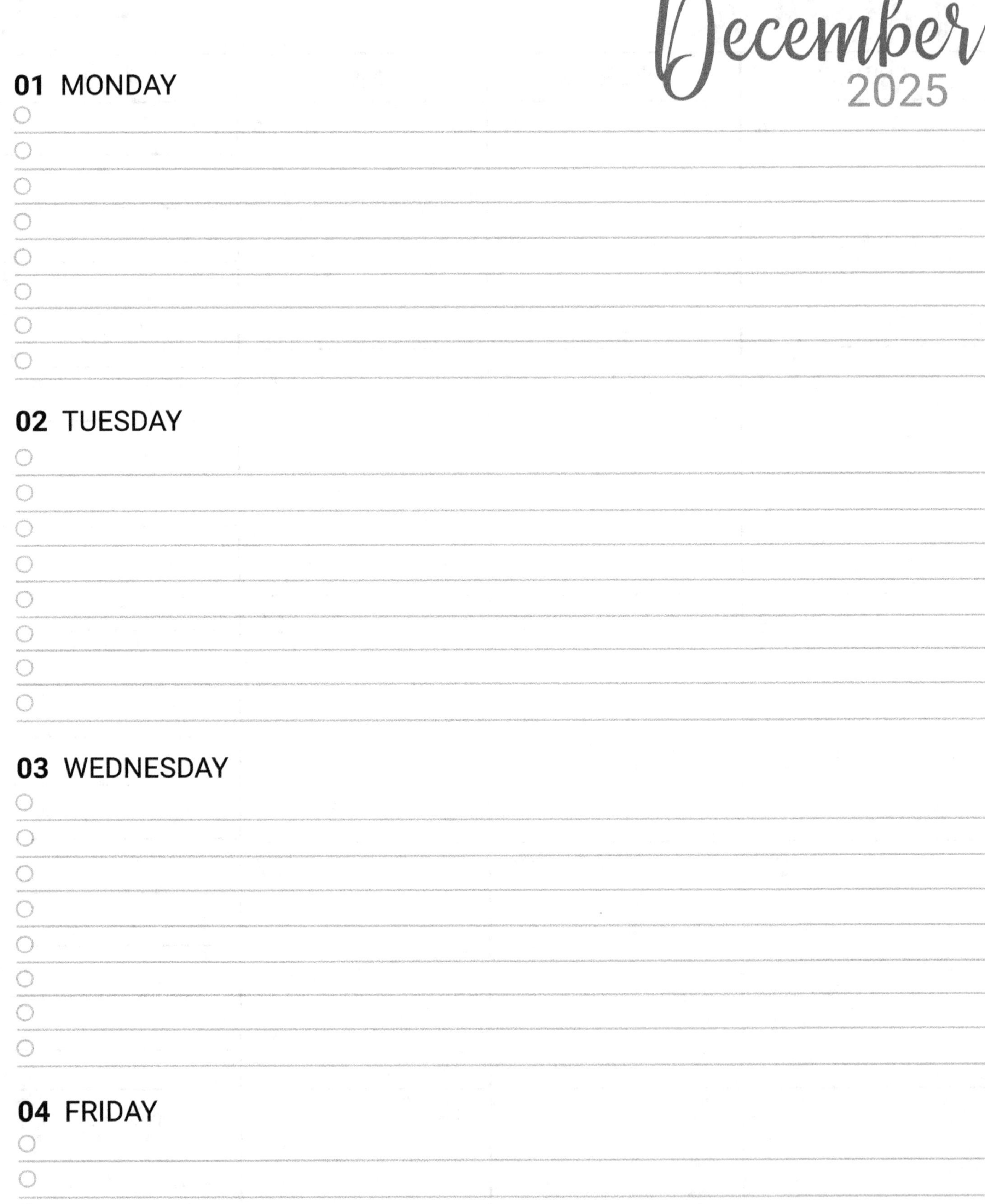

# December
## 2025

**01** MONDAY

**02** TUESDAY

**03** WEDNESDAY

**04** FRIDAY

**05** FRIDAY

**06** SATURDAY

**07** SUNDAY

**08** MONDAY

**09** TUESDAY

**10** WEDNESDAY

**11** THURSDAY

**12** FRIDAY

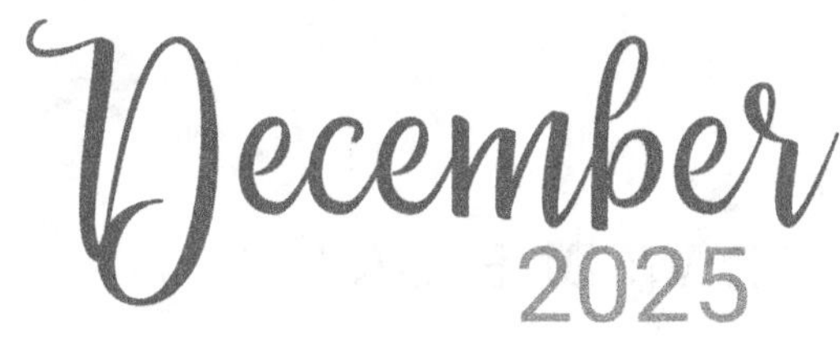



## 13 SATURDAY

## 14 SUNDAY

## 15 MONDAY

## 16 TUESDAY

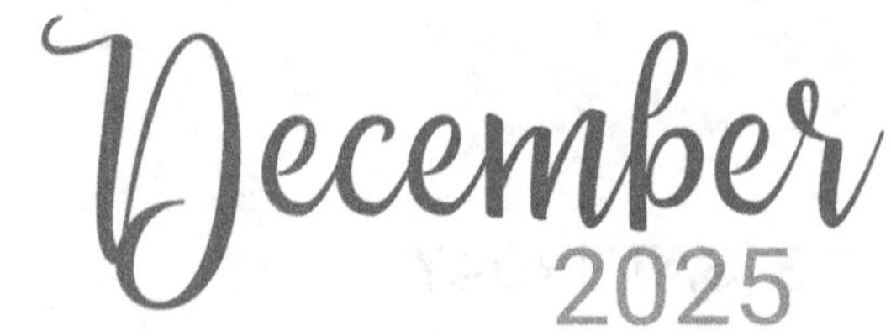

# December
## 2025

**17** WEDNESDAY

**18** THURSDAY

**19** FRIDAY

**20** SATURDAY

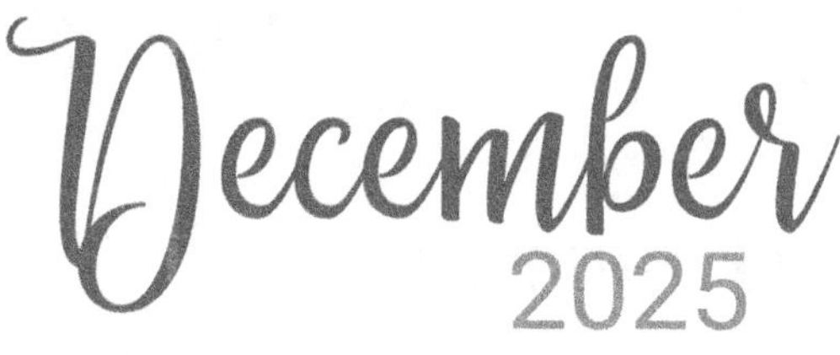


## 21 SUNDAY

## 22 MONDAY

## 23 TUESDAY

## 24 WEDNESDAY

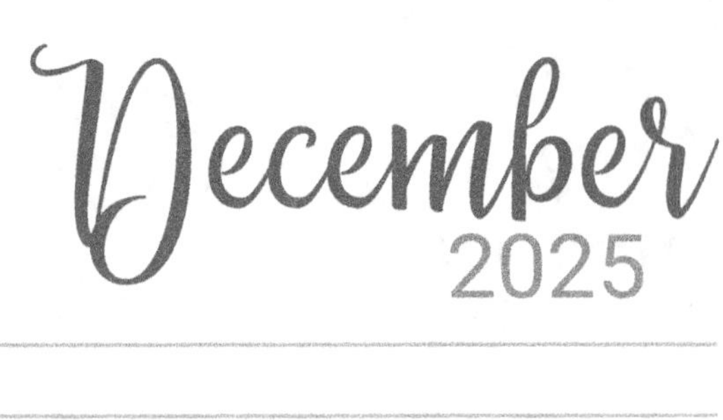

December
2025

**25** THURSDAY

**26** FRIDAY

**27** SATURDAY

**28** SUNDAY

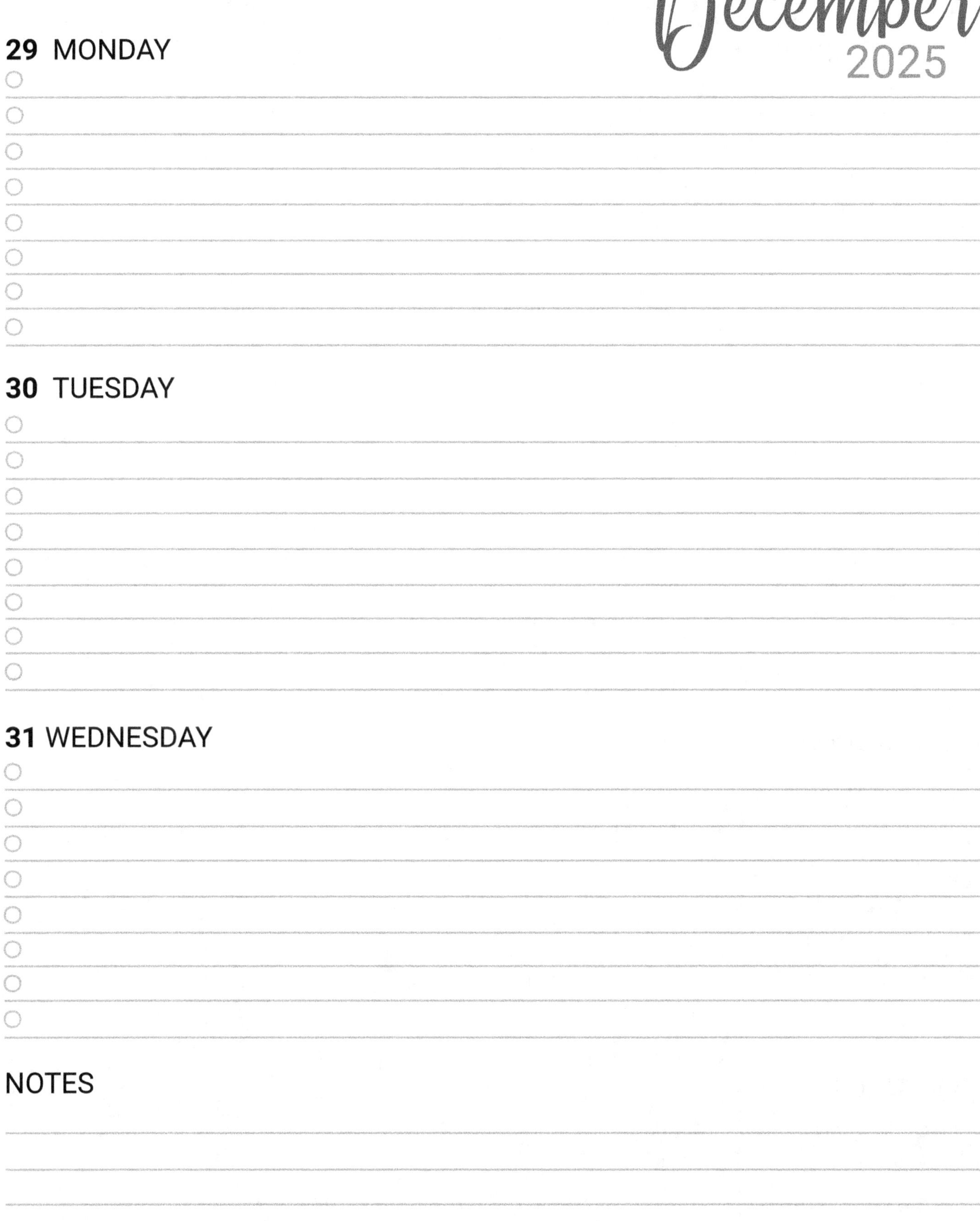

December
2025

29 MONDAY

30 TUESDAY

31 WEDNESDAY

NOTES

# January
## 2026

**01** THURSDAY

**02** FRIDAY

**03** SATURDAY

**04** SUNDAY

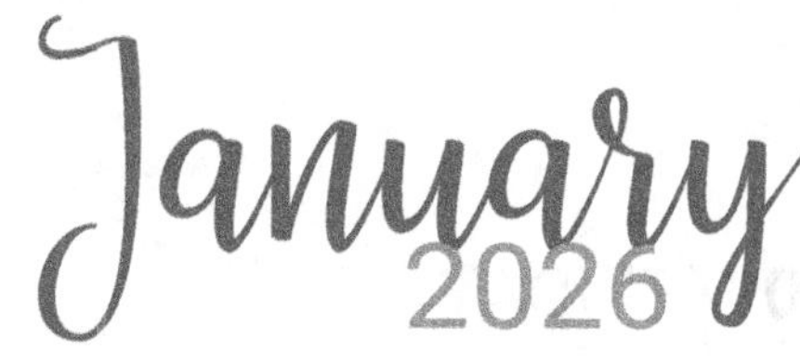

**05** MONDAY

**06** TUESDAY

**07** WEDNESDAY

**08** THURSDAY

**09** FRIDAY

**10** SATURDAY

**11** SUNDAY

**12** MONDAY

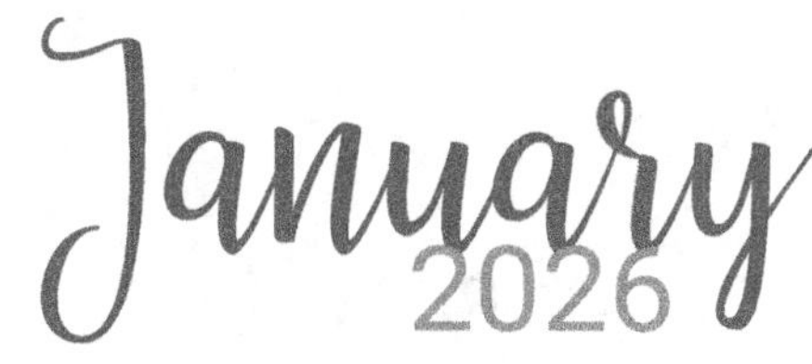

# January
## 2026

**13** TUESDAY

**14** WEDNESDAY

**15** THURSDAY

**16** FRIDAY

## 17 SATURDAY

## 18 SUNDAY

## 19 MONDAY

## 20 TUESDAY

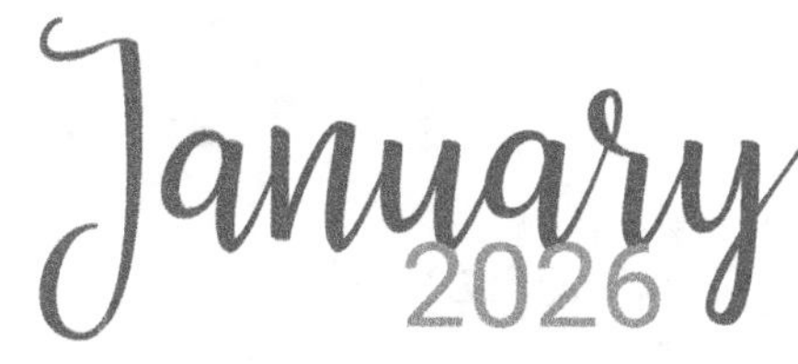


## 21 WEDNESDAY

## 22 THURSDAY

## 23 FRIDAY

## 24 SATURDAY

**25** SUNDAY

**26** MONDAY

**27** TUESDAY

**28** WEDNESDAY

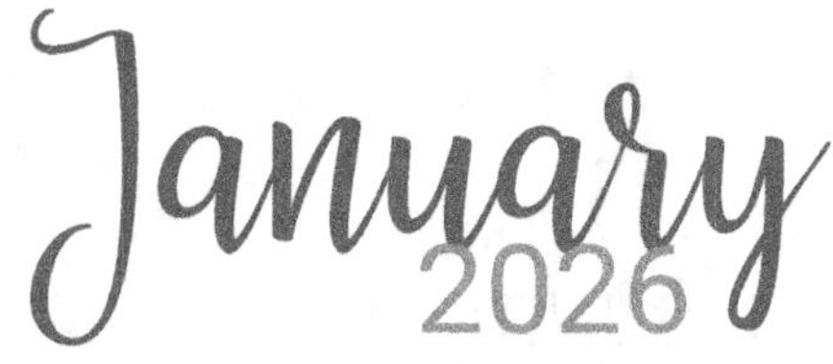


## 29 THURSDAY

## 30 FRIDAY

## 31 SATURDAY

## NOTES

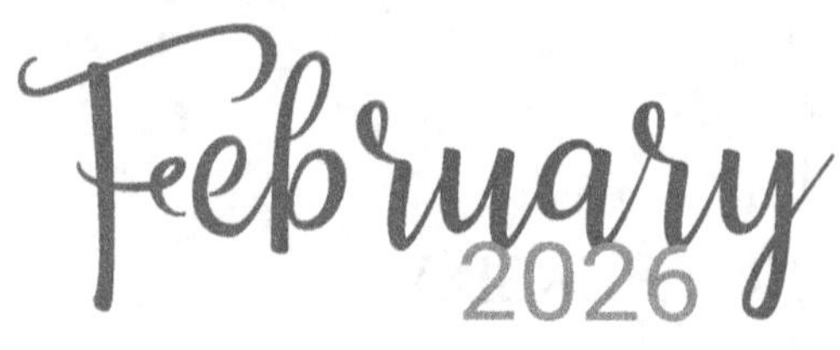



## 01 SUNDAY

## 02 MONDAY

## 03 TUESDAY

## 04 WEDNESDAY

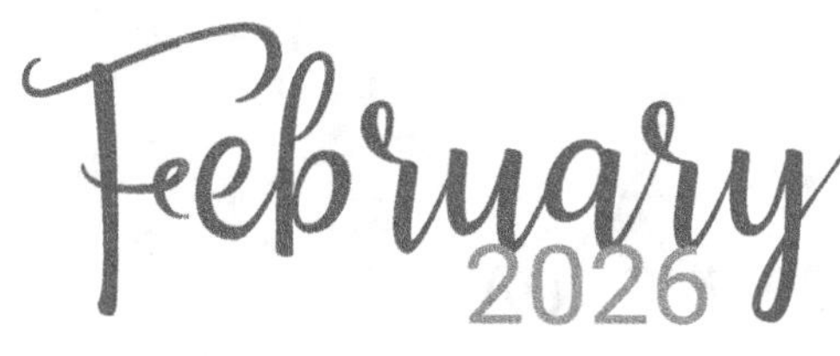


## 05 THURSDAY

## 06 FRIDAY

## 07 SATURDAY

## 08 SUNDAY

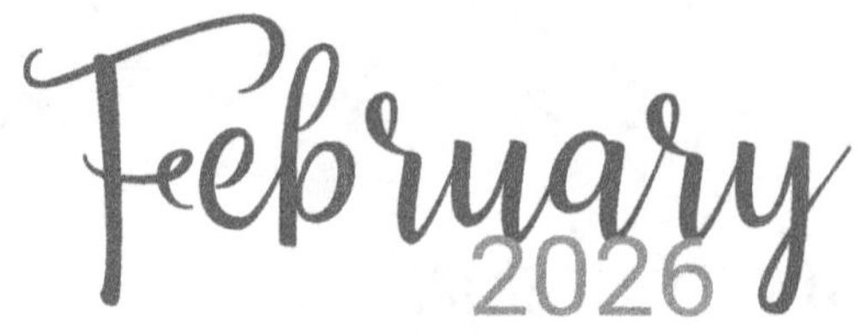


**09** MONDAY

**10** TUESDAY

**11** WEDNESDAY

**12** THURSDAY

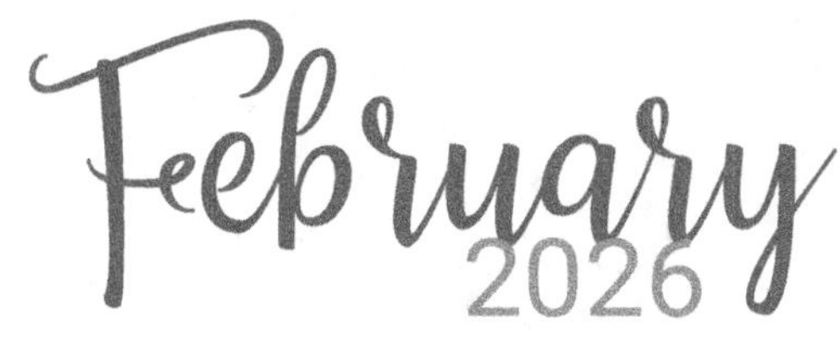


**13** FRIDAY

**14** SATURDAY

**15** SUNDAY

**16** MONDAY

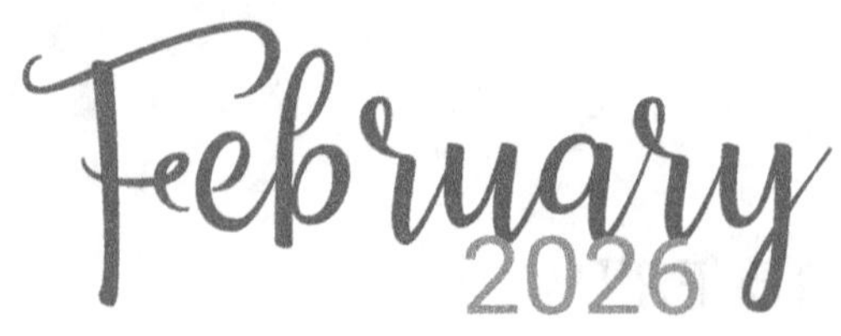


**17** TUESDAY

**18** WEDNESDAY

**19** THURSDAY

**20** FRIDAY

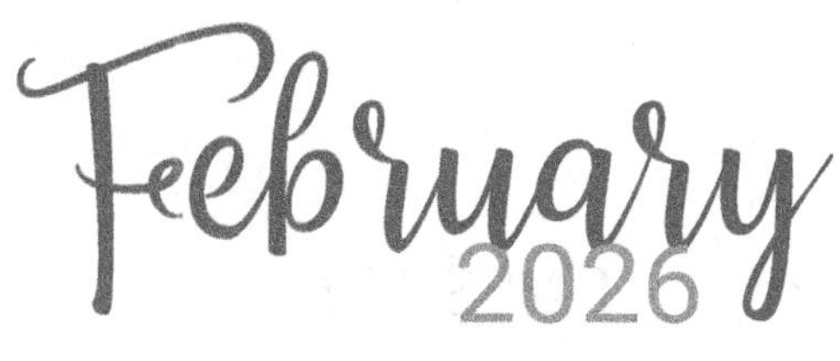

# February
## 2026

**21** SATURDAY

**22** SUNDAY

**23** MONDAY

**24** TUESDAY

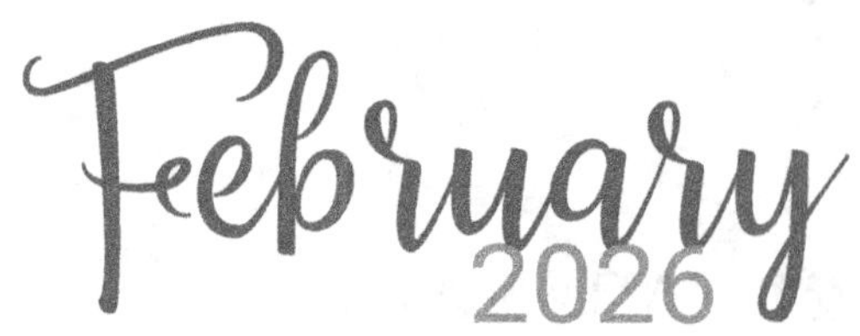

# February
## 2026

**25** WEDNESDAY

**26** THURSDAY

**27** FRIDAY

**28** SATURDAY

# March
## 2026

**01** SUNDAY

**02** MONDAY

**03** TUESDAY

**04** WEDNESDAY

# March 2026

## 05 THURSDAY

## 06 FRIDAY

## 07 SATURDAY

## 08 SUNDAY

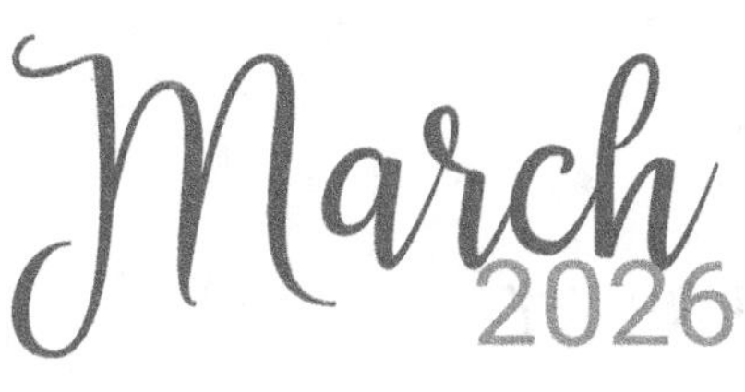



**09** MONDAY

**10** TUESDAY

**11** WEDNESDAY

**12** THURSDAY

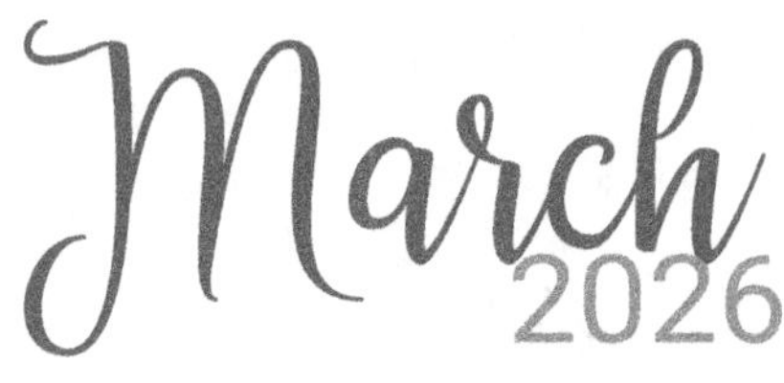



**13** FRIDAY

**14** SATURDAY

**15** SUNDAY

**16** MONDAY

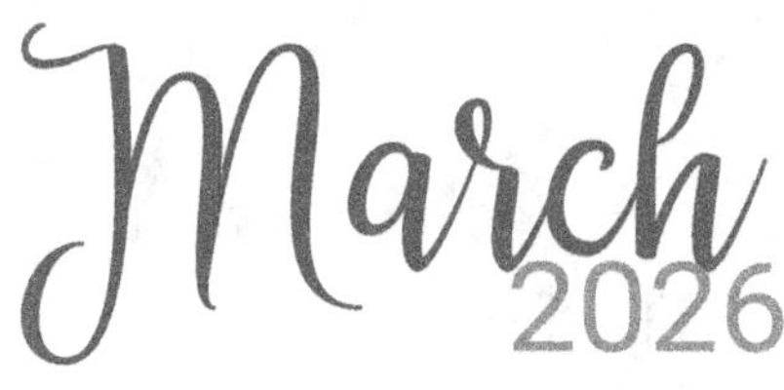


**17** TUESDAY

**18** WEDNESDAY

**19** THURSDAY

**20** FRIDAY

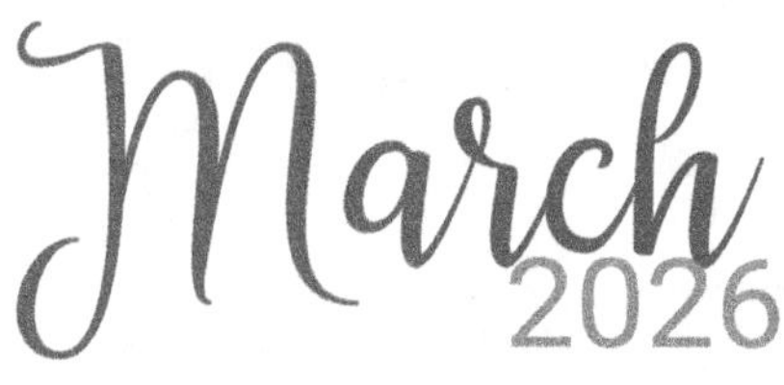


**21** SATURDAY

**22** SUNDAY

**23** MONDAY

**24** TUESDAY

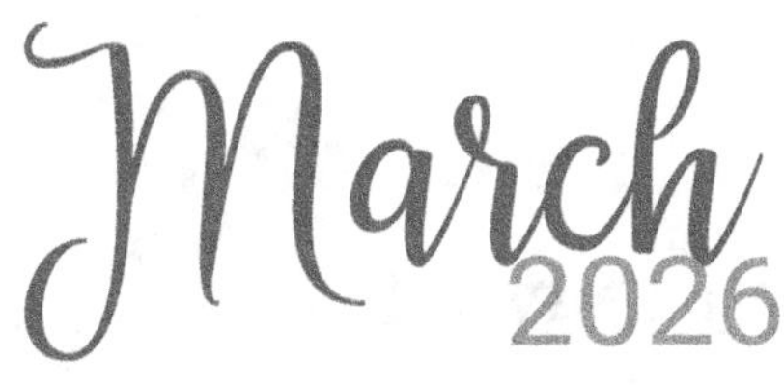


## 25 WEDNESDAY

## 26 THURSDAY

## 27 FRIDAY

## 28 SATURDAY

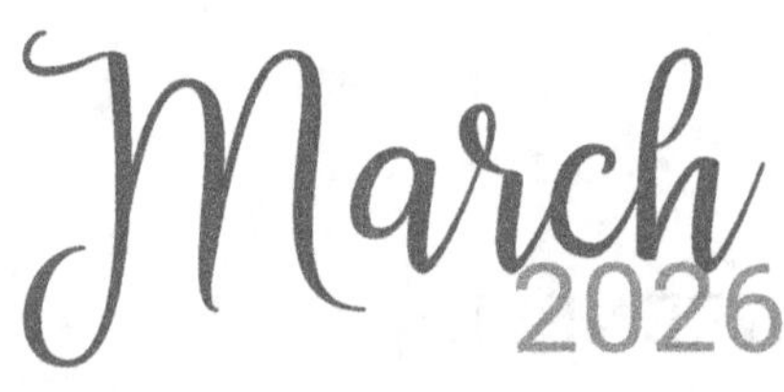

**29** SUNDAY

**30** MONDAY

**31** TUESDAY

NOTES

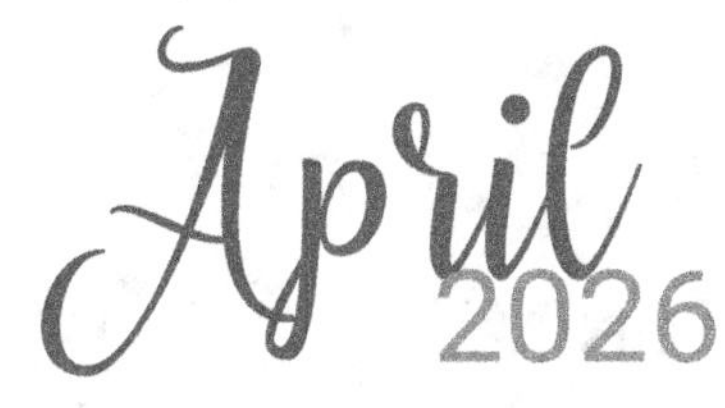


**01** WEDNESDAY

**02** THURSDAY

**03** FRIDAY

**04** SATURDAY

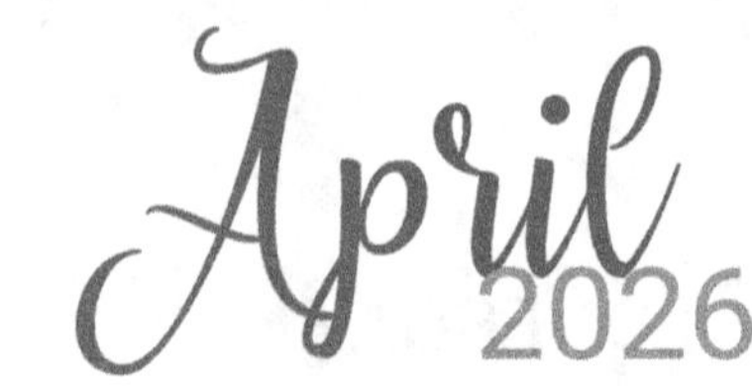

# April
## 2026

**05** SUNDAY

**06** MONDAY

**07** TUESDAY

**08** WEDNESDAY

## 09 THURSDAY

## 10 FRIDAY

## 11 SATURDAY

## 12 SUNDAY

## 13 MONDAY

## 14 TUESDAY

## 15 WEDNESDAY

## 16 THURSDAY

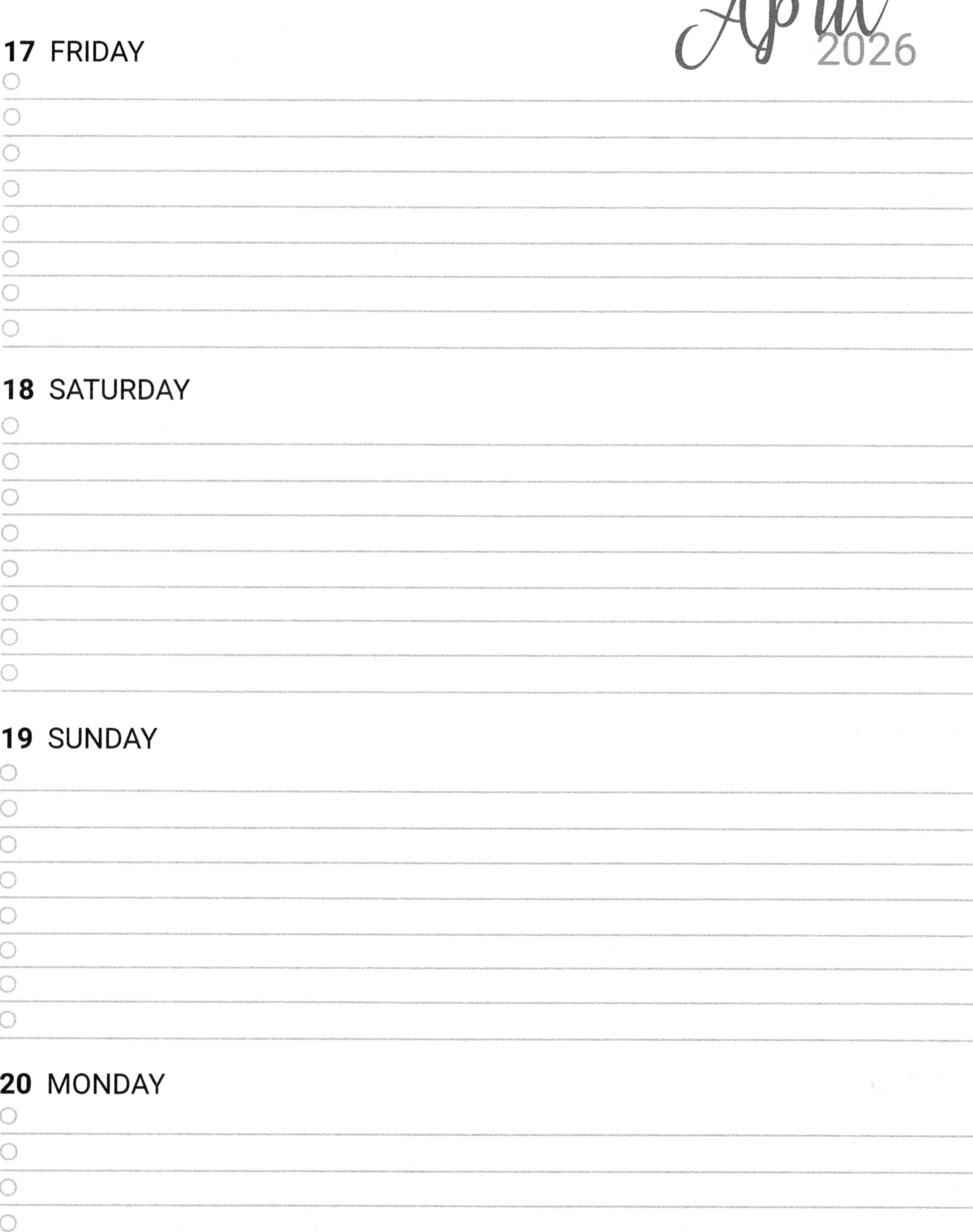



**17** FRIDAY

**18** SATURDAY

**19** SUNDAY

**20** MONDAY

**21** TUESDAY

**22** WEDNESDAY

**23** THURSDAY

**24** FRIDAY

**25** SATURDAY

**26** SUNDAY

**27** MONDAY

**28** TUESDAY

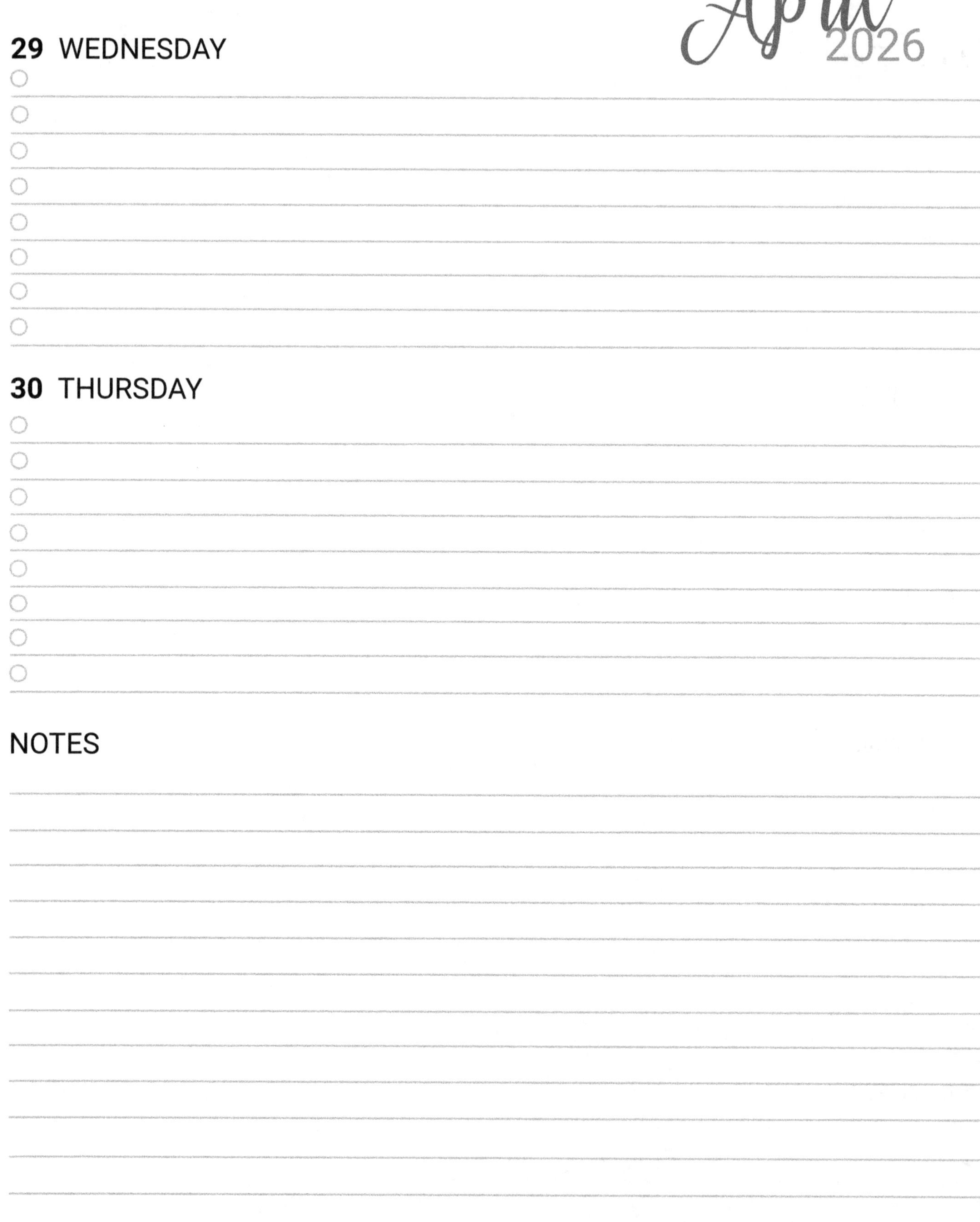



## 29 WEDNESDAY

## 30 THURSDAY

## NOTES

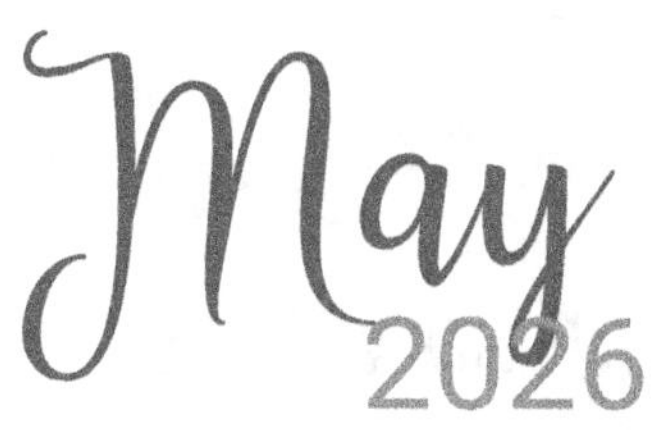


## 01 FRIDAY

## 02 SATURDAY

## 03 SUNDAY

## 04 MONDAY

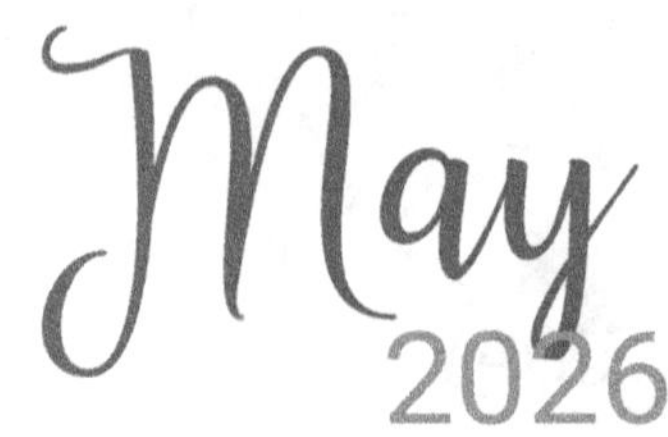

# May
## 2026

**05** TUESDAY

**06** WEDNESDAY

**07** THURSDAY

**08** FRIDAY

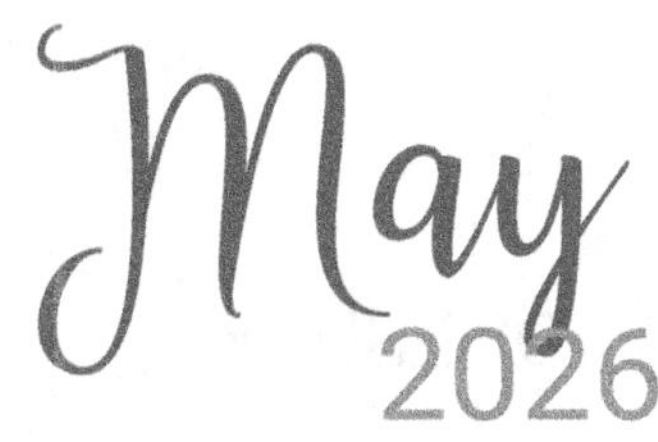


**09** SATURDAY

**10** SUNDAY

**11** MONDAY

**12** TUESDAY

**13** WEDNESDAY

**14** THURSDAY

**15** FRIDAY

**16** SATURDAY

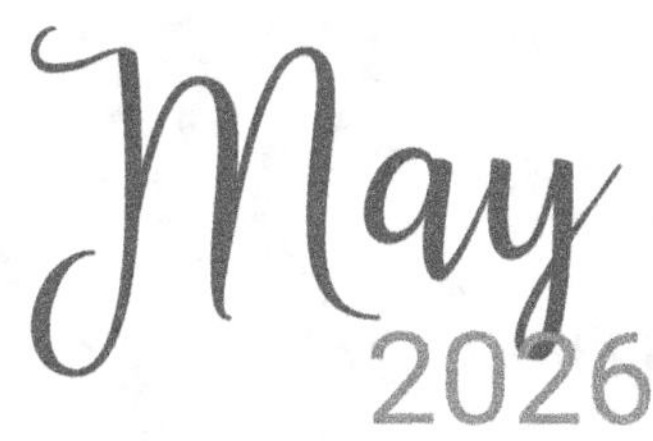


## 17 SUNDAY

## 18 MONDAY

## 19 TUESDAY

## 20 WEDNESDAY

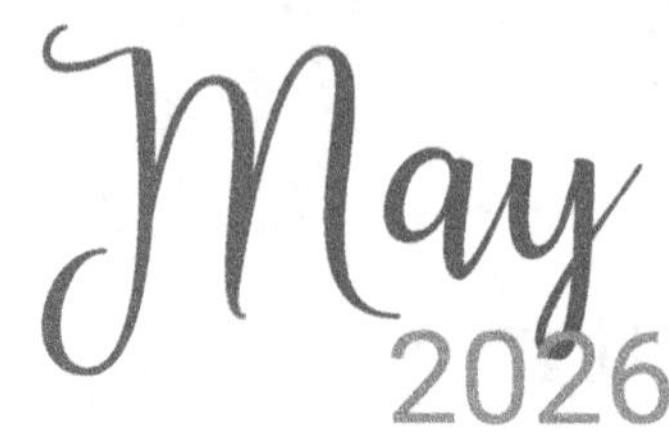

# May
## 2026

## 21 THURSDAY

## 22 FRIDAY

## 23 SATURDAY

## 24 SUNDAY

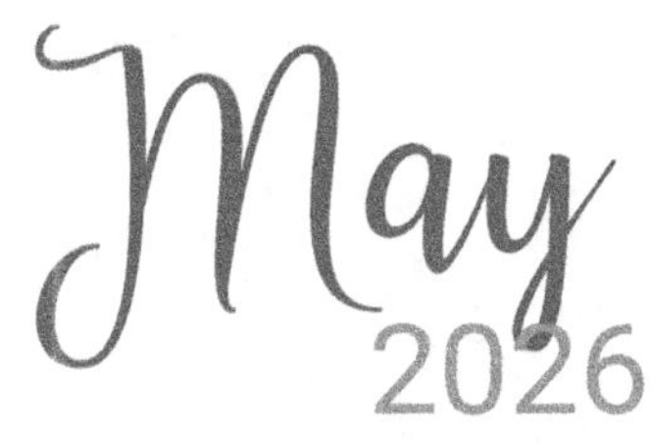



**25** MONDAY

**26** TUESDAY

**27** WEDNESDAY

**28** THURSDAY

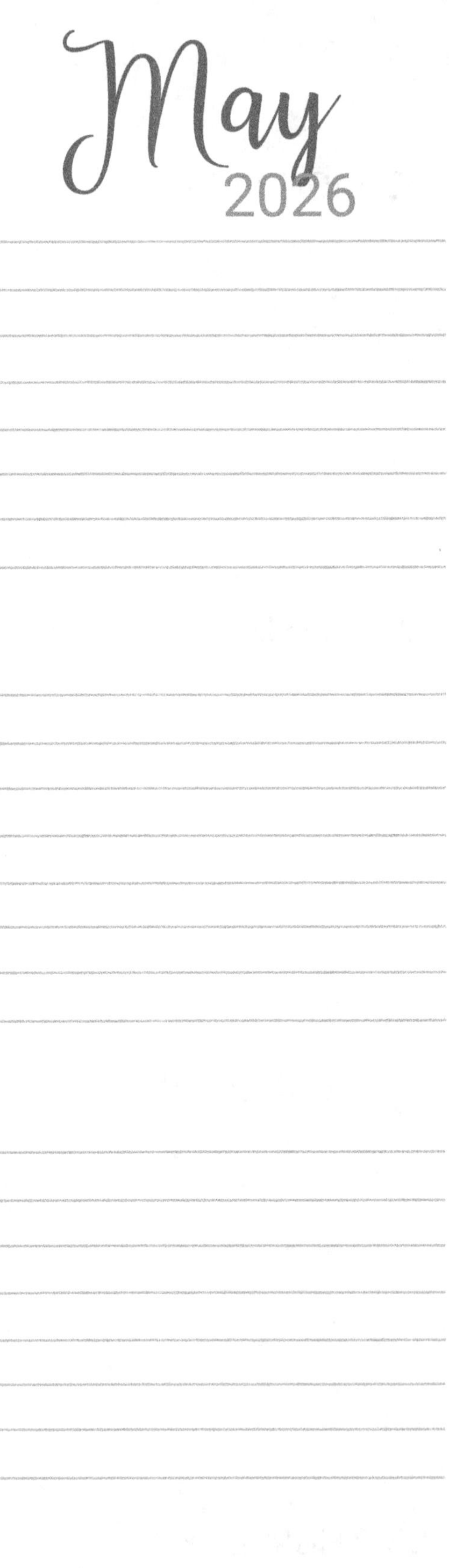

# May 2026

**29** FRIDAY

**30** SATURDAY

**31** SUNDAY

NOTES

**01** MONDAY

**02** TUESDAY

**03** WEDNESDAY

**04** THURSDAY

June
2026

**05** FRIDAY

**06** SATURDAY

**07** SUNDAY

**08** MONDAY

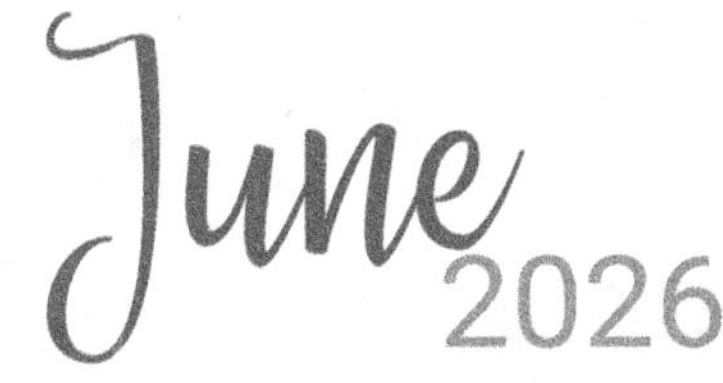


**09** TUESDAY

**10** WEDNESDAY

**11** THURSDAY

**12** FRIDAY

**13** SATURDAY

**14** SUNDAY

**15** MONDAY

**16** TUESDAY

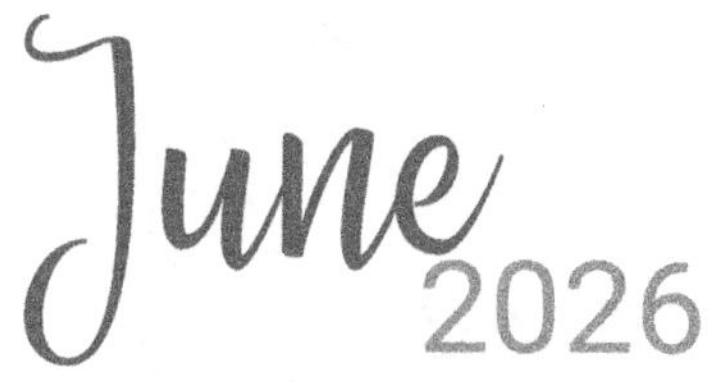


**17** WEDNESDAY

**18** THURSDAY

**19** FRIDAY

**20** SATURDAY

# June 2026

**21** SUNDAY

**22** MONDAY

**23** TUESDAY

**24** WEDNESDAY

## 25 THURSDAY

## 26 FRIDAY

## 27 SATURDAY

## 28 SUNDAY

**29** MONDAY

**30** TUESDAY

NOTES

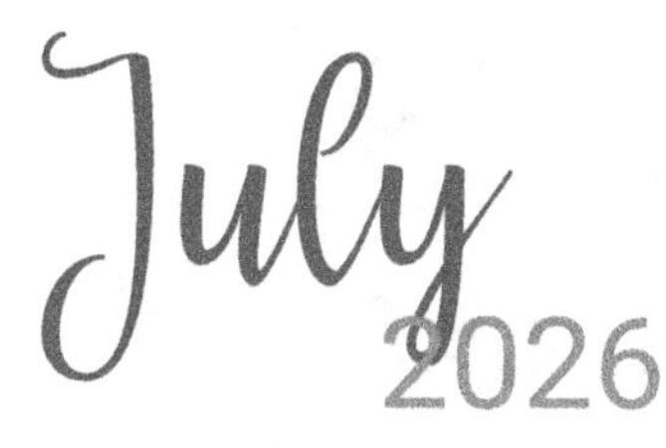

# July 2026

## 01 WEDNESDAY

## 02 THURSDAY

## 03 FRIDAY

## 04 SATURDAY

**05** SUNDAY

**06** MONDAY

**07** TUESDAY

**08** WEDNESDAY

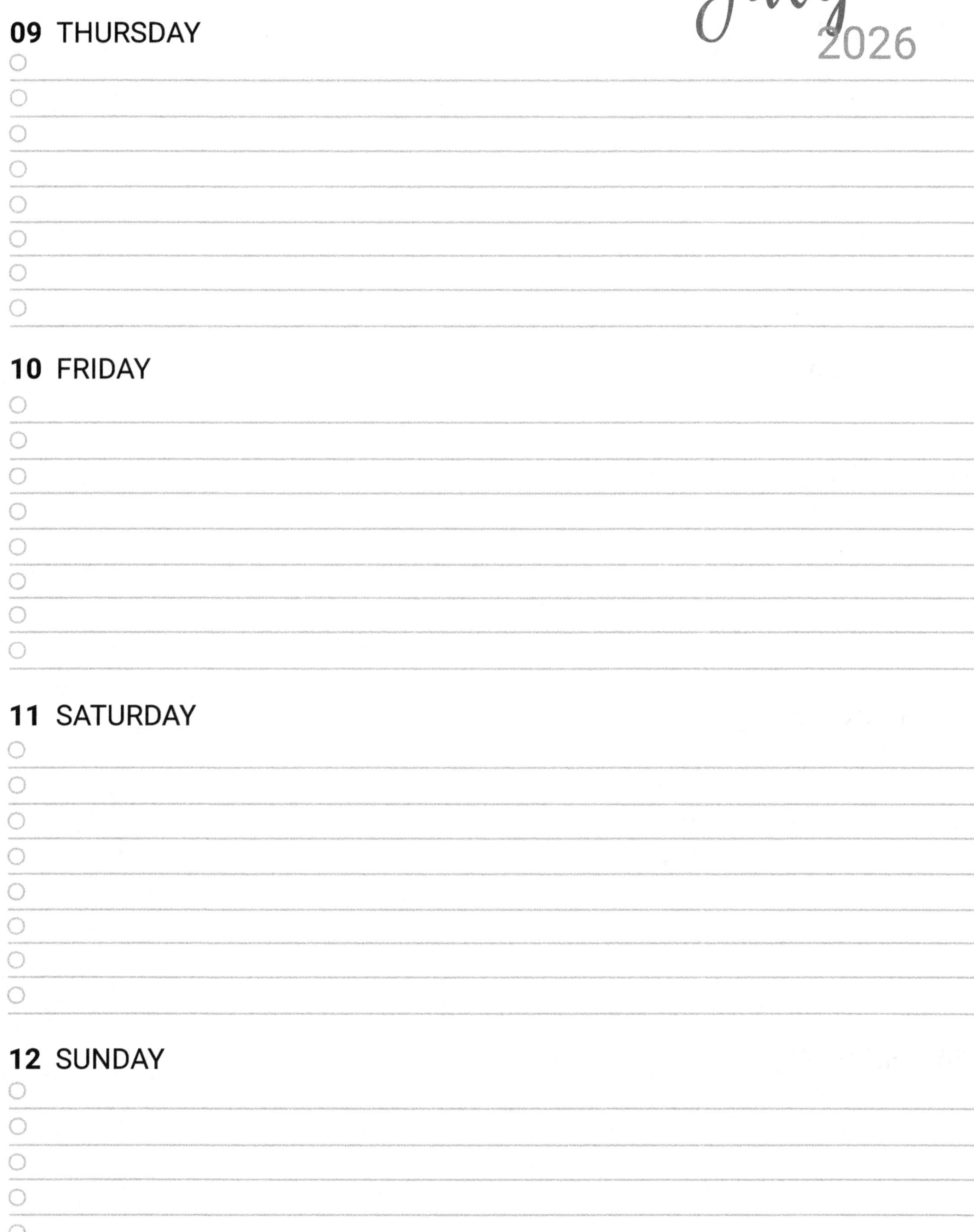



**09** THURSDAY

**10** FRIDAY

**11** SATURDAY

**12** SUNDAY

**13** MONDAY

**14** TUESDAY

**15** WEDNESDAY

**16** THURSDAY

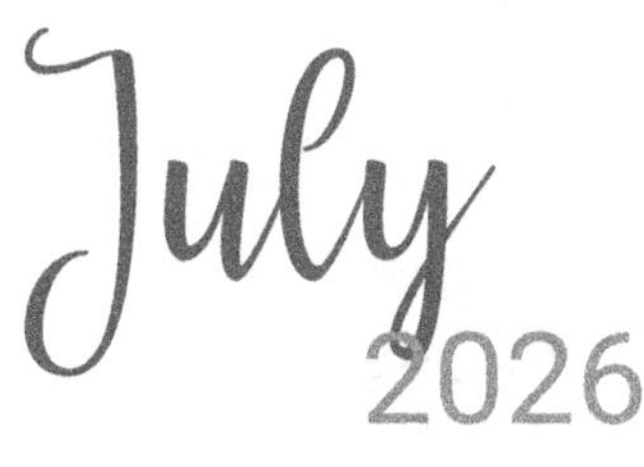

# July
## 2026

**17** FRIDAY

**18** SATURDAY

**19** SUNDAY

**20** MONDAY

**21** TUESDAY

**22** WEDNESDAY

**23** THURSDAY

**24** FRIDAY

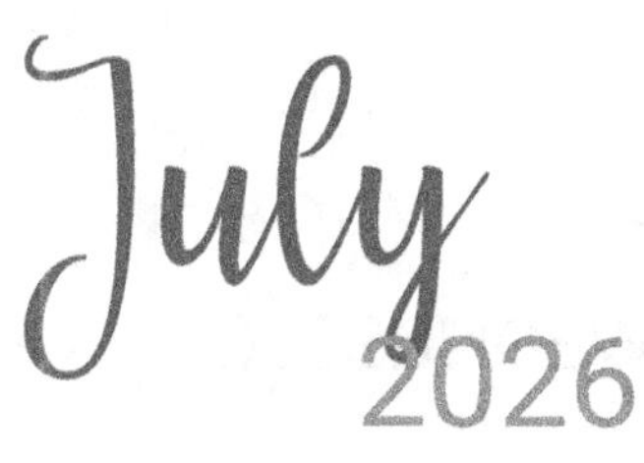

# July 2026

**25** SATURDAY

**26** SUNDAY

**27** MONDAY

**28** TUESDAY

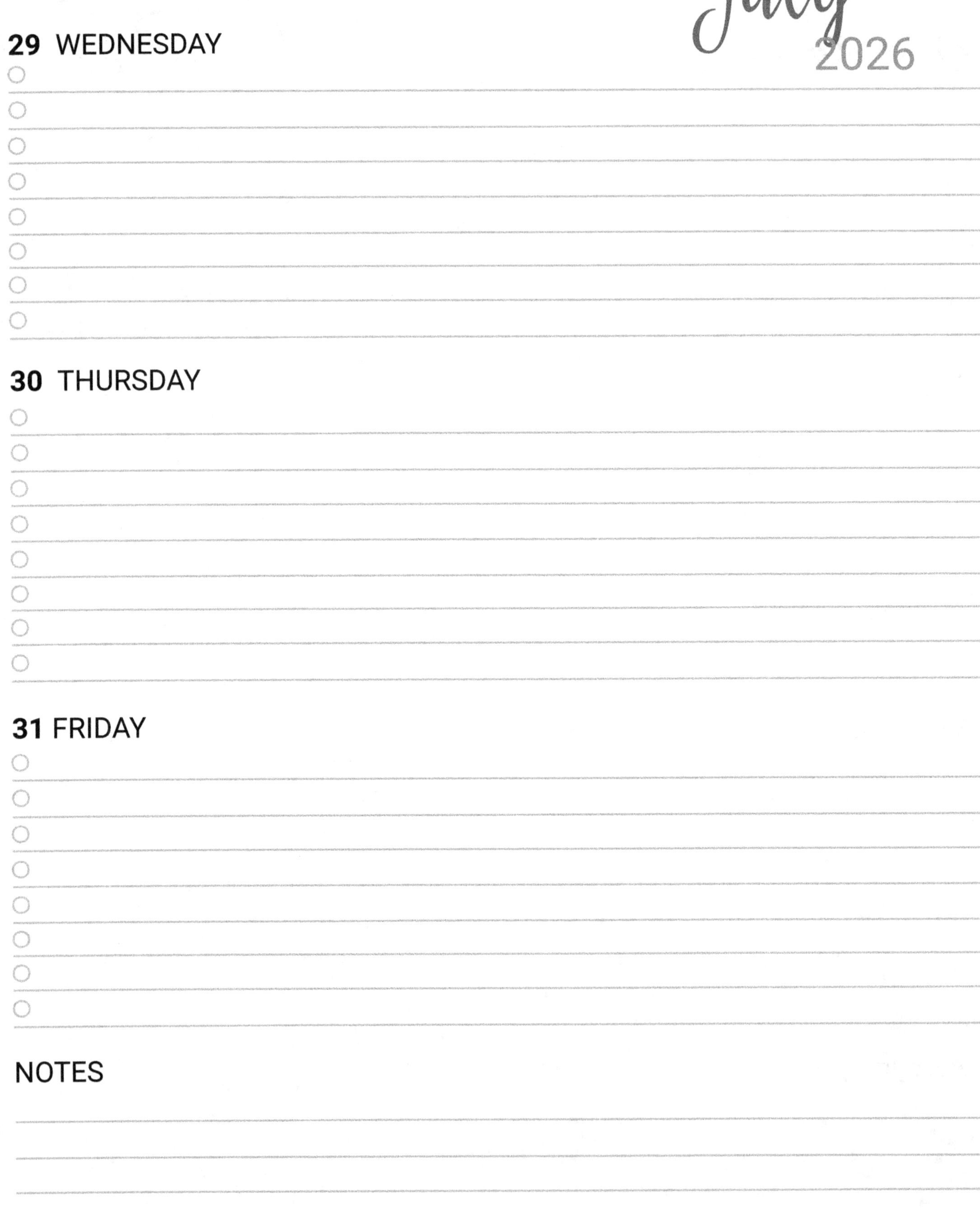


July
2026

29 WEDNESDAY

30 THURSDAY

31 FRIDAY

NOTES

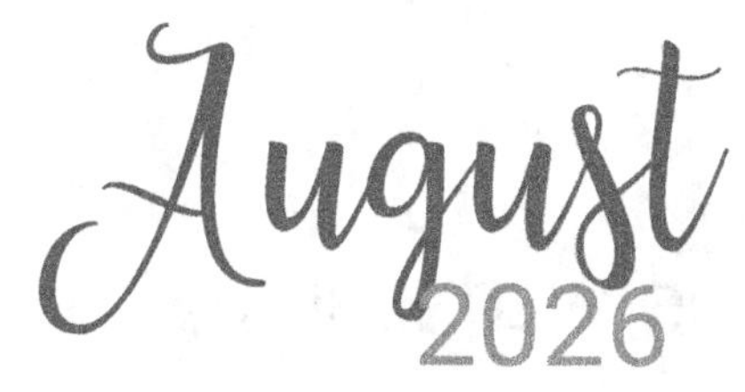



## 01 SATURDAY

## 02 SUNDAY

## 03 MONDAY

## 04 TUESDAY

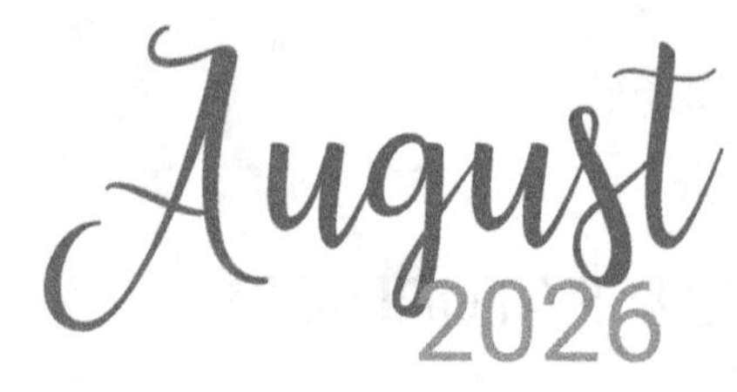


## 05 WEDNESDAY

## 06 THURSDAY

## 07 FRIDAY

## 08 SATURDAY

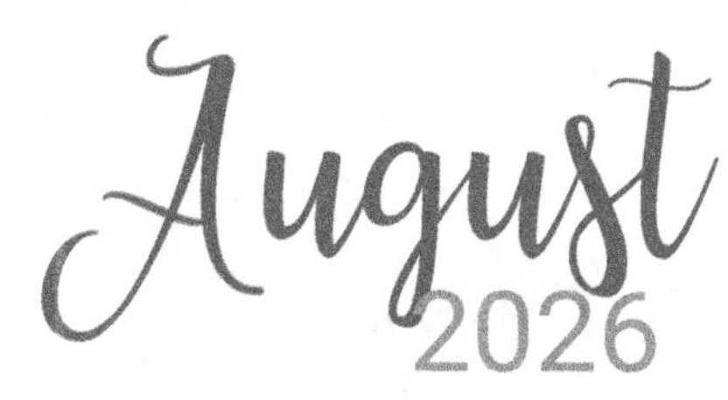


## 09 SUNDAY

## 10 MONDAY

## 11 TUESDAY

## 12 WEDNESDAY

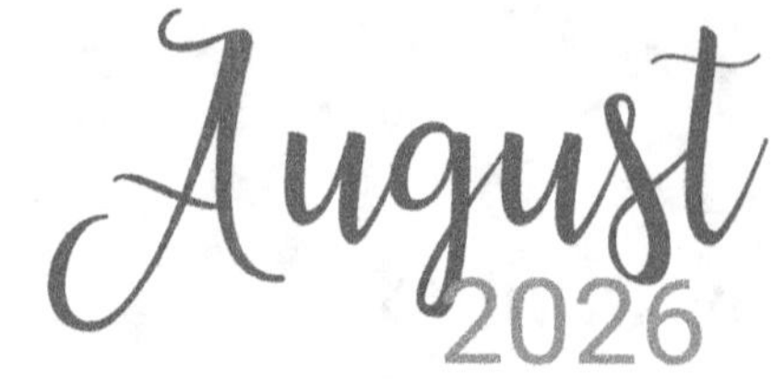



**13** THURSDAY

**14** FRIDAY

**15** SATURDAY

**16** SUNDAY

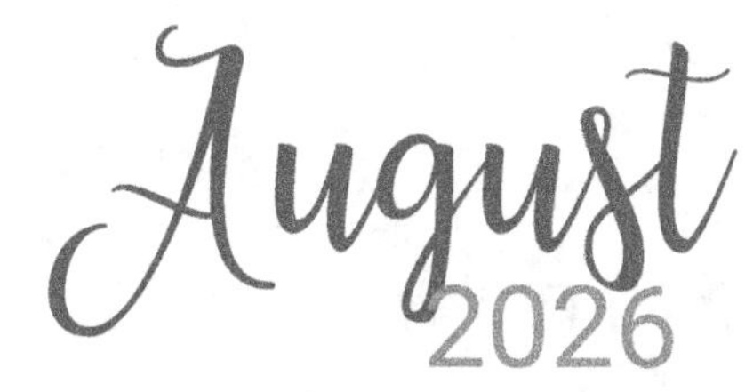



**17** MONDAY

**18** TUESDAY

**19** WEDNESDAY

**20** THURSDAY

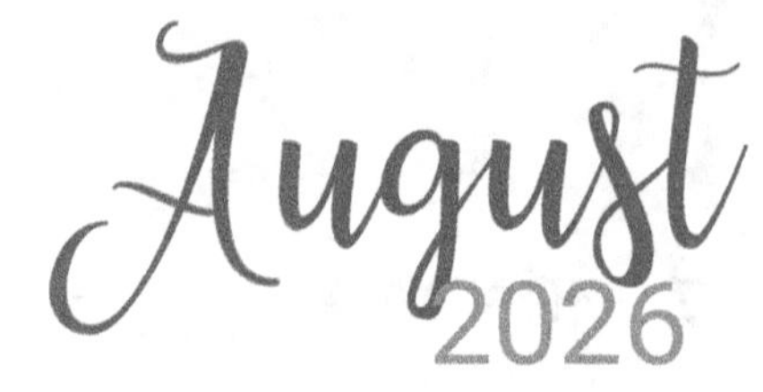


## 21 FRIDAY

## 22 SATURDAY

## 23 SUNDAY

## 24 MONDAY

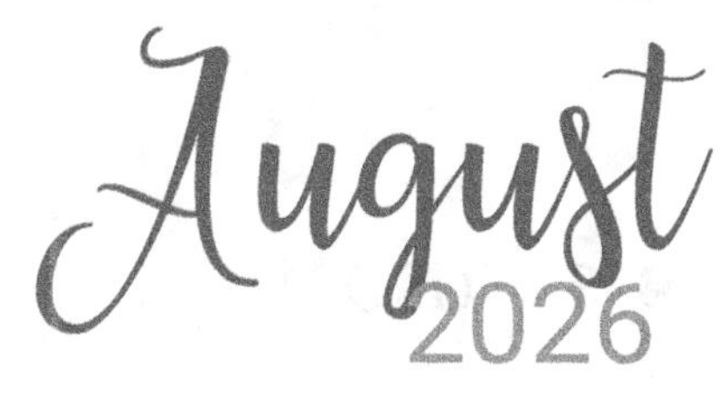



## 25 TUESDAY

## 26 WEDNESDAY

## 27 THURSDAY

## 28 FRIDAY

## 29 SATURDAY

## 30 SUNDAY

## 31 MONDAY

## NOTES

**01** TUESDAY

**02** WEDNESDAY

**03** THURSDAY

**04** FRIDAY

**05** SATURDAY

**06** SUNDAY

**07** MONDAY

**08** TUESDAY

**09** WEDNESDAY

**10** THURSDAY

**11** FRIDAY

**12** SATURDAY

## 13 SUNDAY

## 14 MONDAY

## 15 TUESDAY

## 16 WEDNESDAY

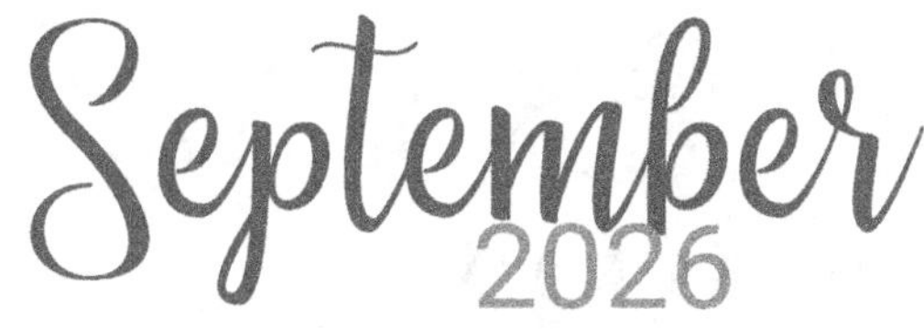


**17** THURSDAY

**18** FRIDAY

**19** SATURDAY

**20** SUNDAY

**21** MONDAY

**22** TUESDAY

**23** WEDNESDAY

**24** THURSDAY

## 25 FRIDAY

○

○

○

○

○

○

○

○

## 26 SATURDAY

○

○

○

○

○

○

○

○

## 27 SUNDAY

○

○

○

○

○

○

○

○

## 28 MONDAY

○

○

○

○

○

**29** TUESDAY

**30** WEDNESDAY

NOTES

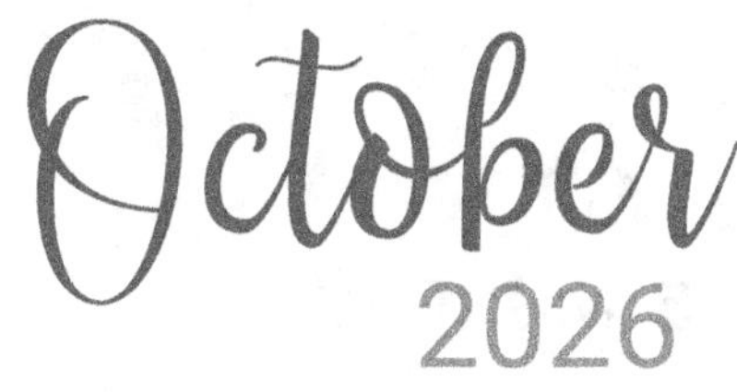



**01** THURSDAY

**02** FRIDAY

**03** SATURDAY

**04** SUNDAY

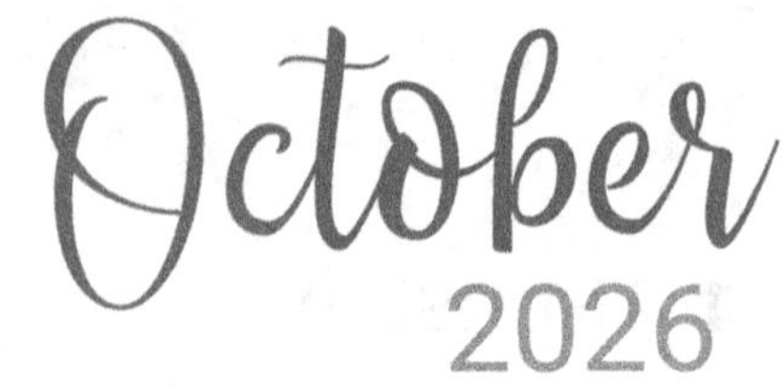



## 05 MONDAY

## 06 TUESDAY

## 07 WEDNESDAY

## 08 THURSDAY

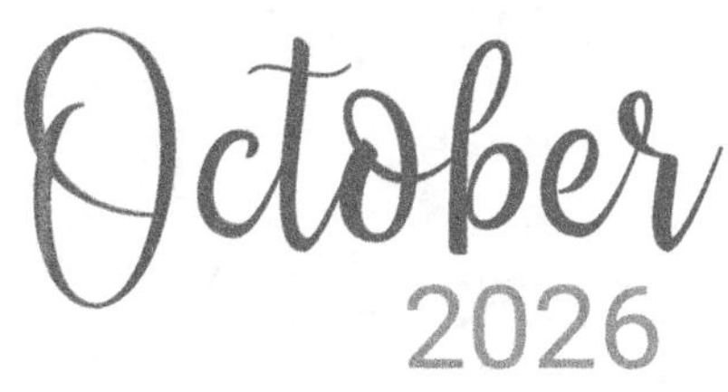



**09** FRIDAY

**10** SATURDAY

**11** SUNDAY

**12** MONDAY

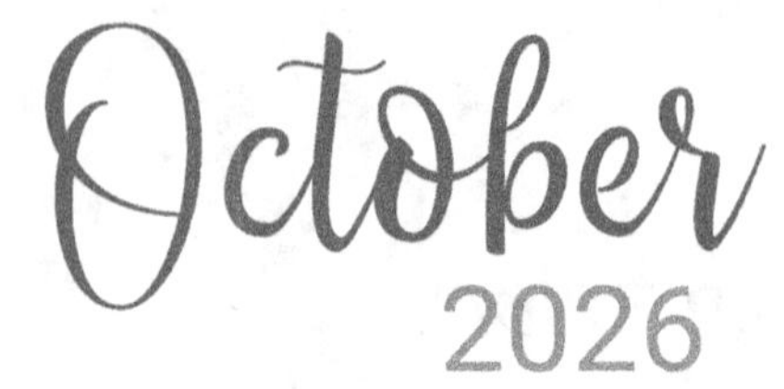


**13** TUESDAY

**14** WEDNESDAY

**15** THURSDAY

**16** FRIDAY

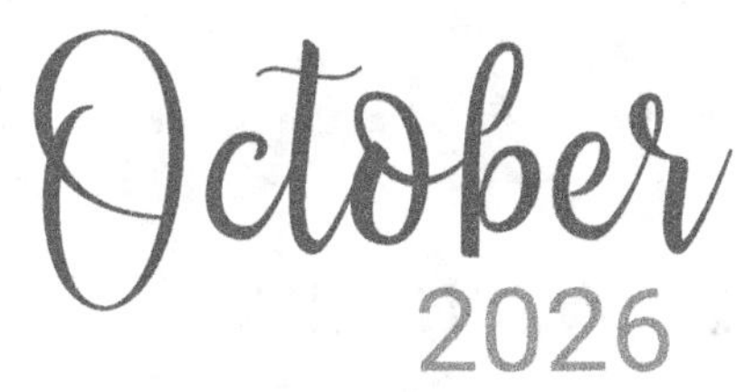



**17** SATURDAY

**18** SUNDAY

**19** MONDAY

**20** TUESDAY

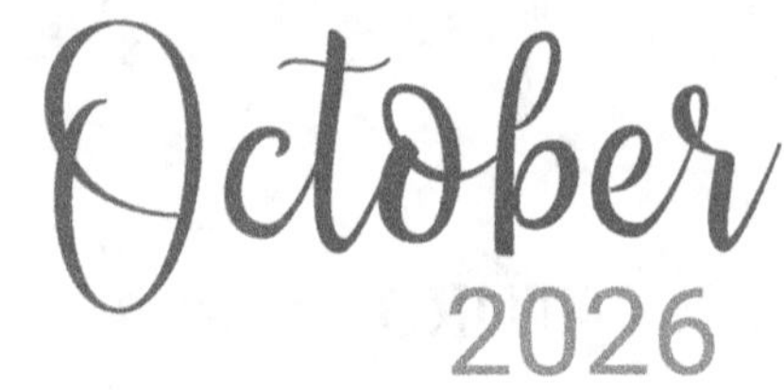

# October
## 2026

**21** WEDNESDAY

**22** THURSDAY

**23** FRIDAY

**24** SATURDAY

# October
## 2026

**25** SUNDAY

**26** MONDAY

**27** TUESDAY

**28** WEDNESDAY

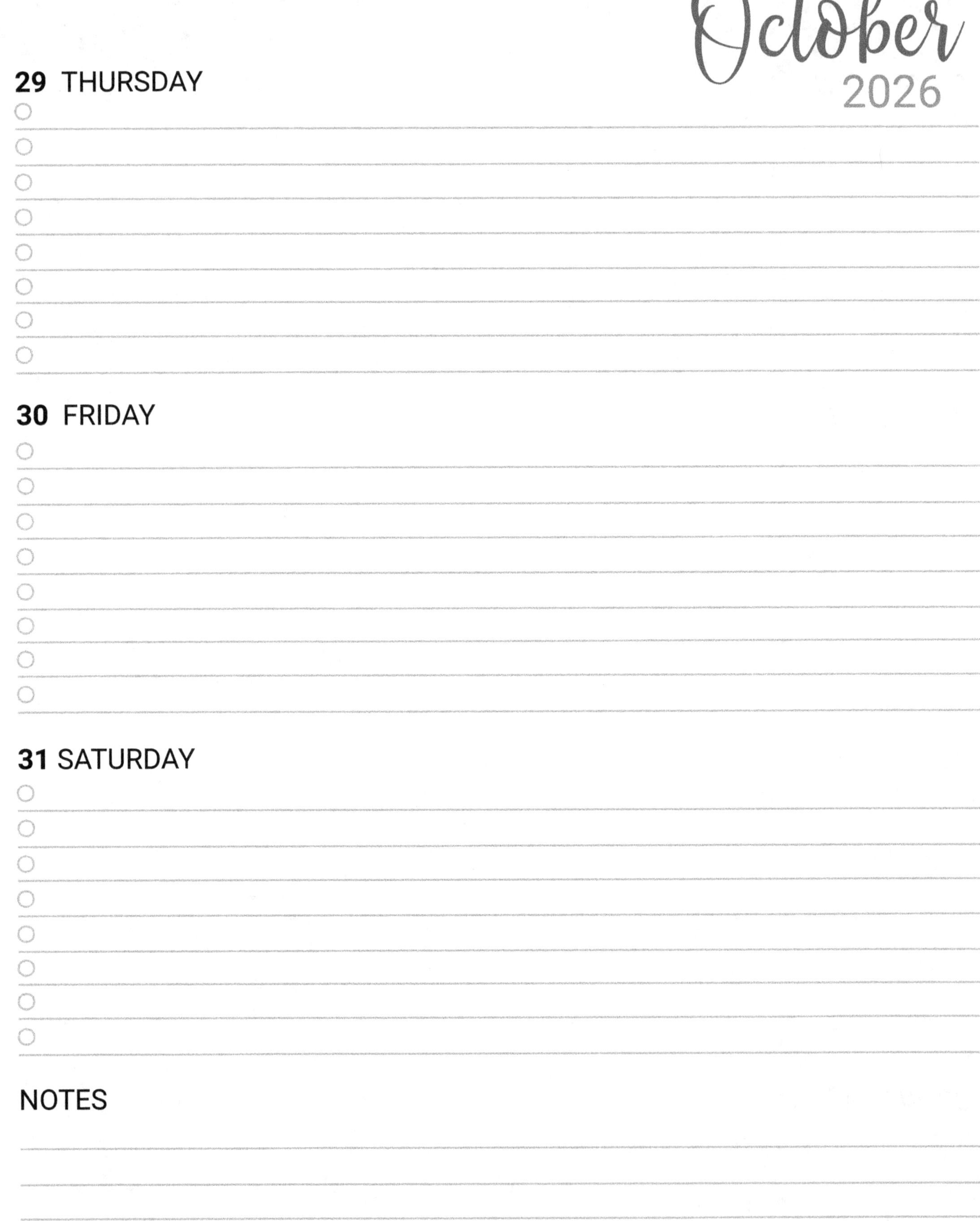

# *October*
## 2026

**29** THURSDAY

**30** FRIDAY

**31** SATURDAY

NOTES

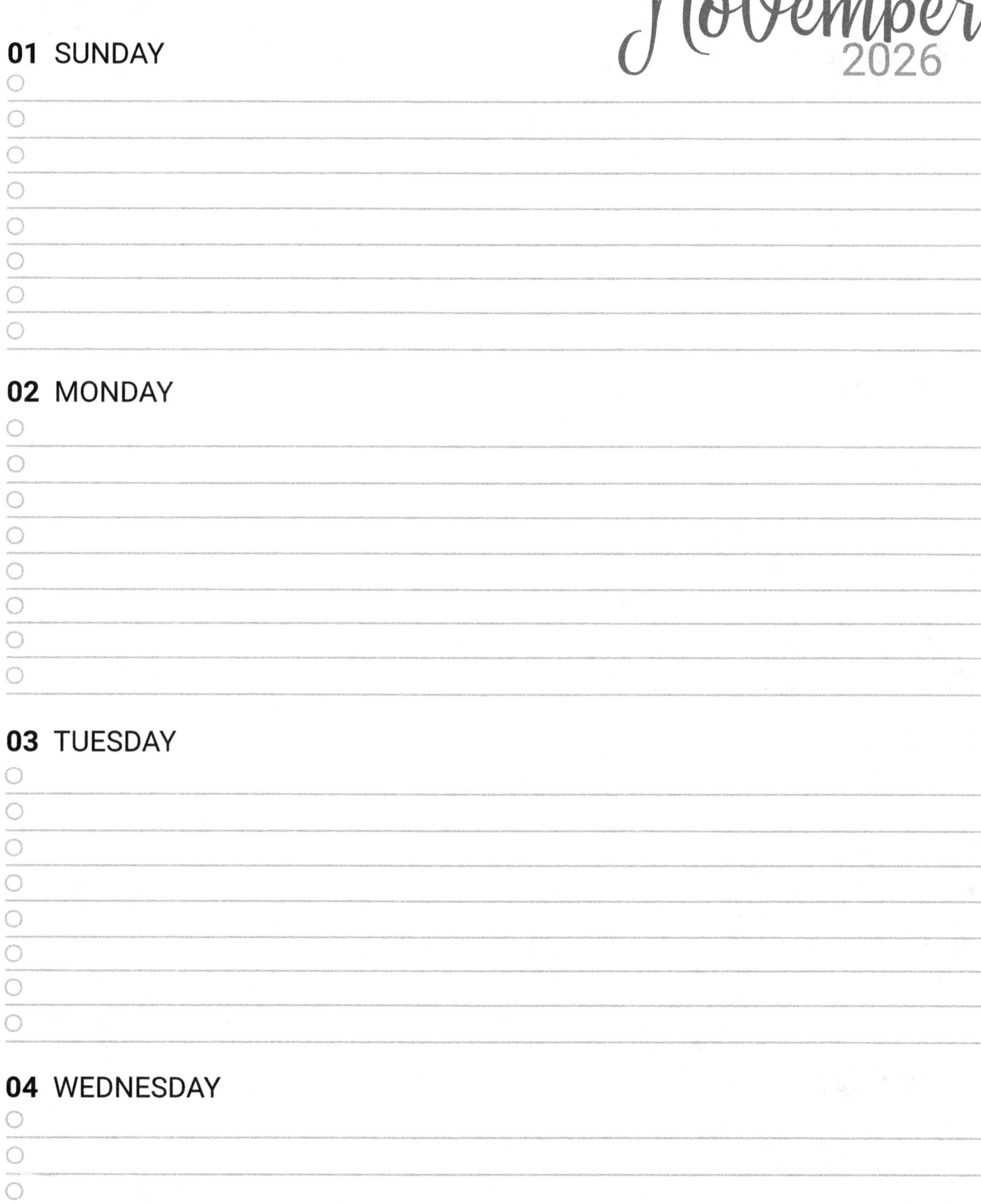
November
2026

01 SUNDAY

02 MONDAY

03 TUESDAY

04 WEDNESDAY

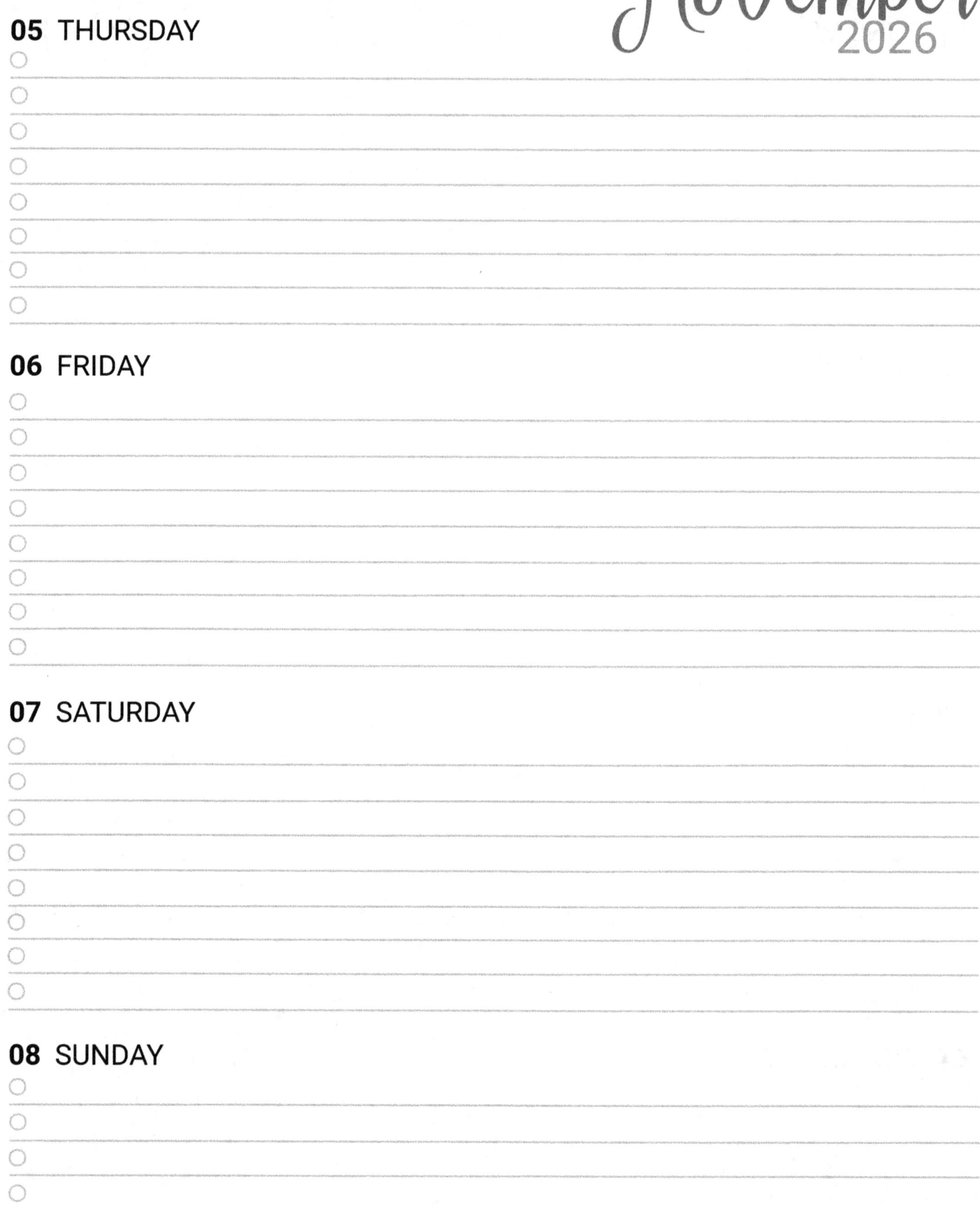



**05** THURSDAY

**06** FRIDAY

**07** SATURDAY

**08** SUNDAY

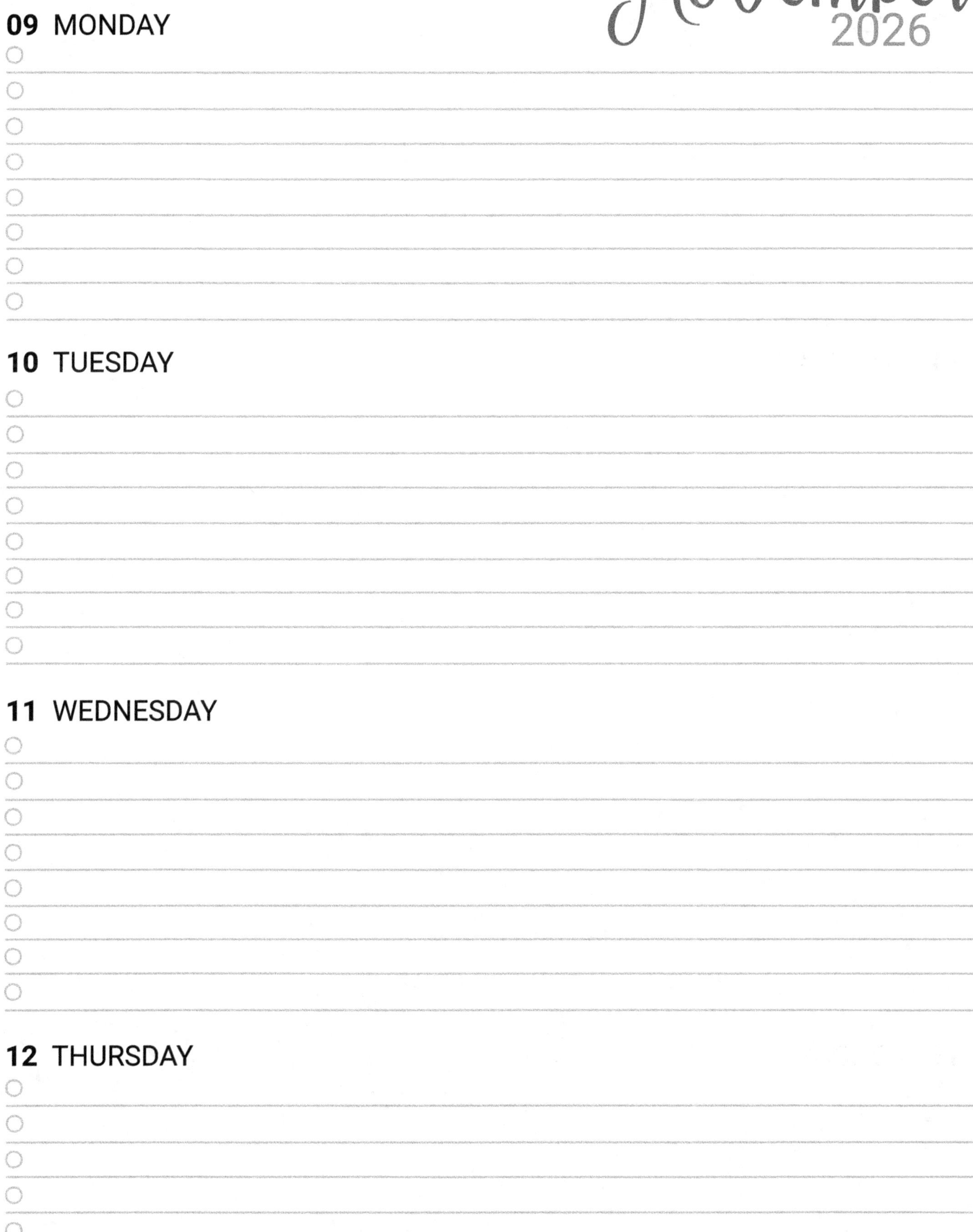



**09** MONDAY

**10** TUESDAY

**11** WEDNESDAY

**12** THURSDAY

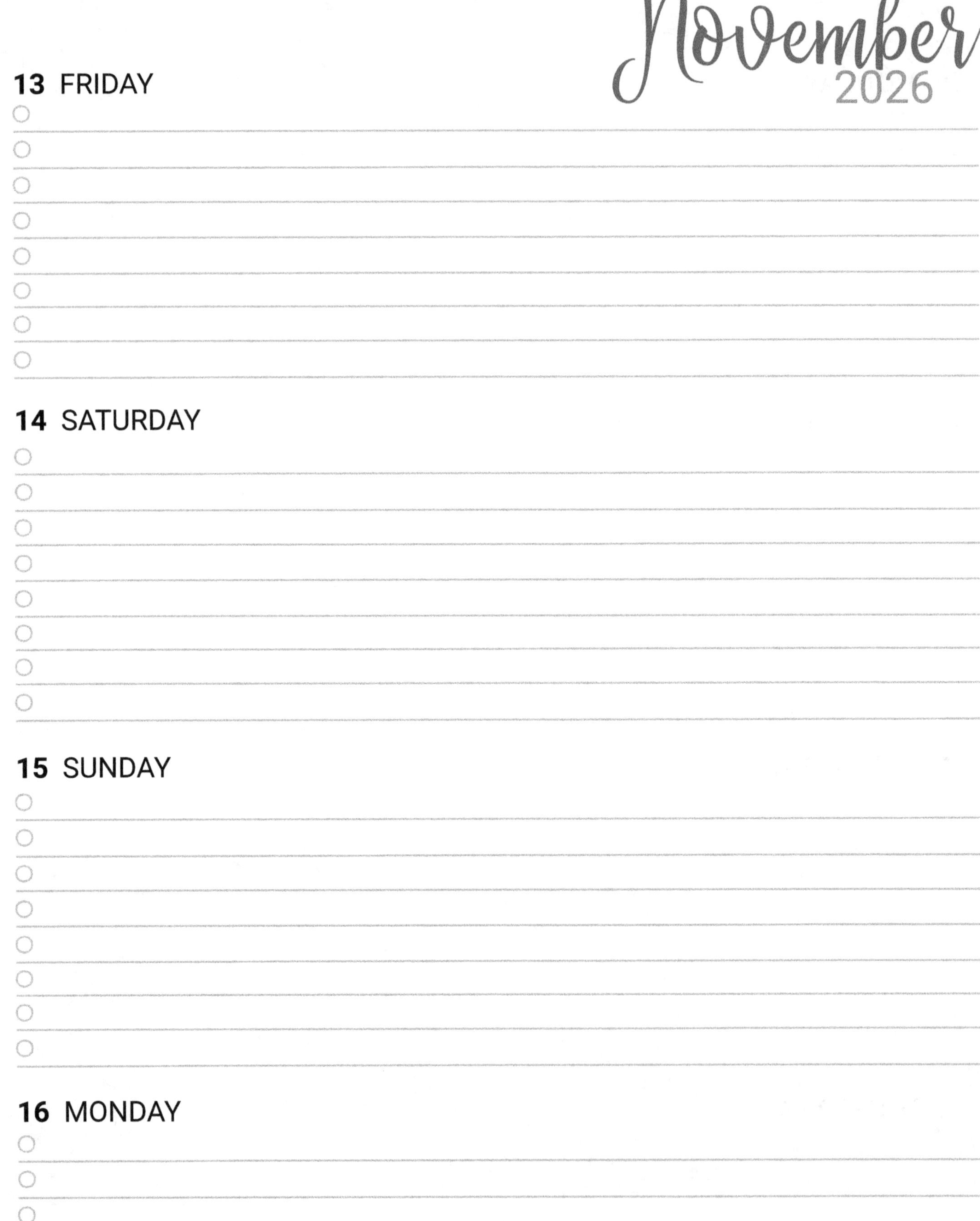



**13** FRIDAY

**14** SATURDAY

**15** SUNDAY

**16** MONDAY

**17** TUESDAY

**18** WEDNESDAY

**19** THURSDAY

**20** FRIDAY

**21** SATURDAY

**22** SUNDAY

**23** MONDAY

**24** TUESDAY

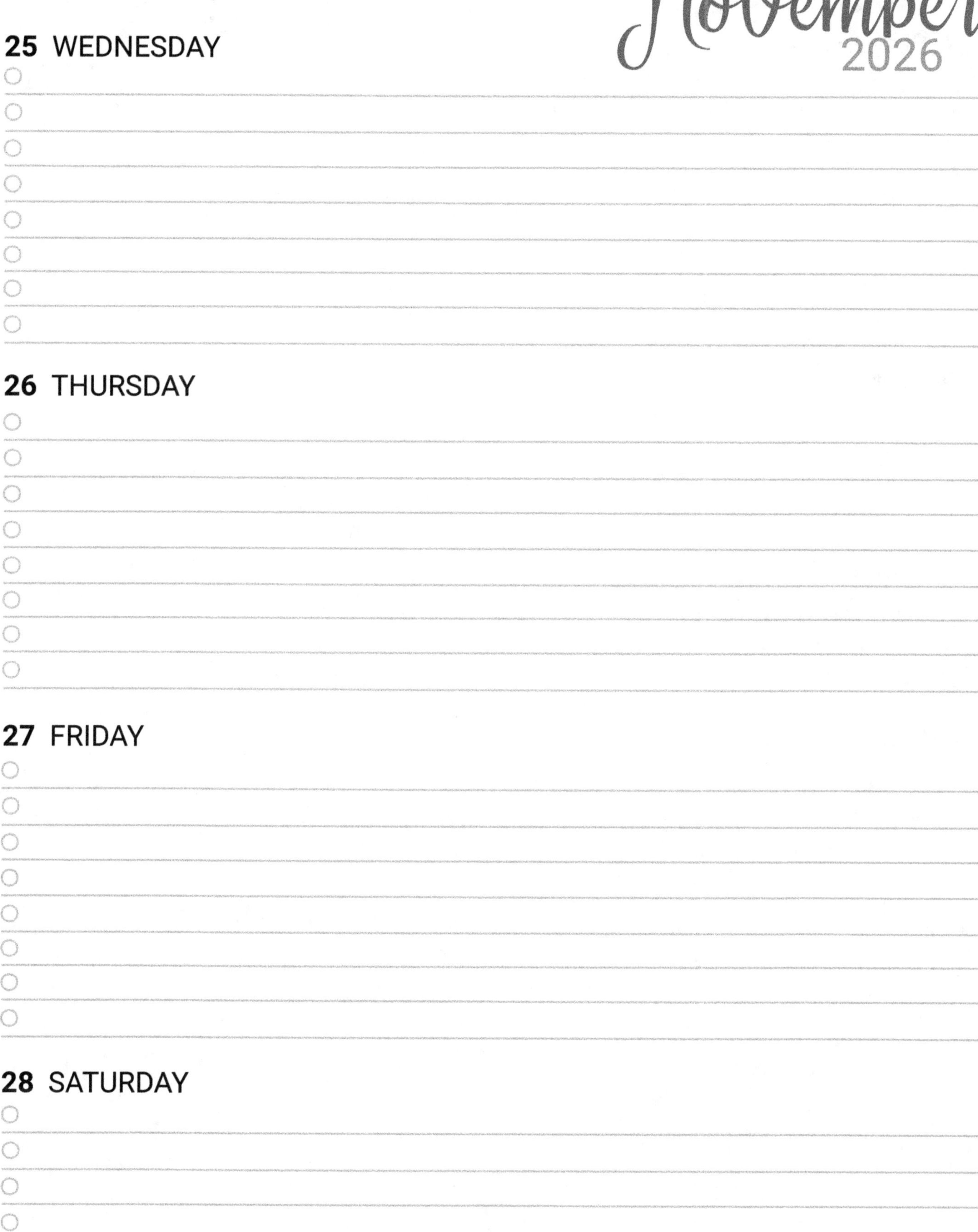



**25** WEDNESDAY

**26** THURSDAY

**27** FRIDAY

**28** SATURDAY

**29** SUNDAY

**30** MONDAY

NOTES

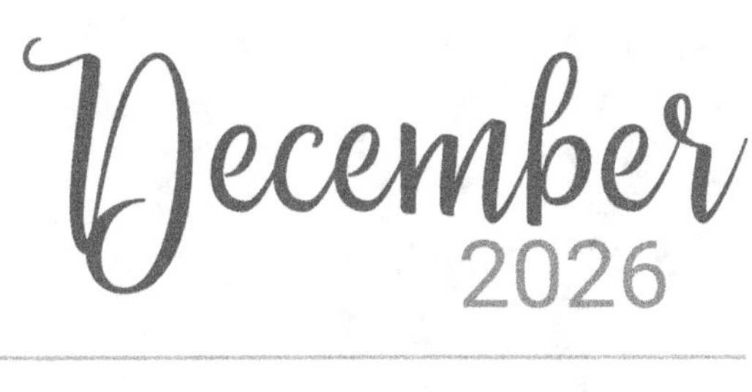

# December
## 2026

**01** TUESDAY

**02** WEDNESDAY

**03** THURSDAY

**04** FRIDAY

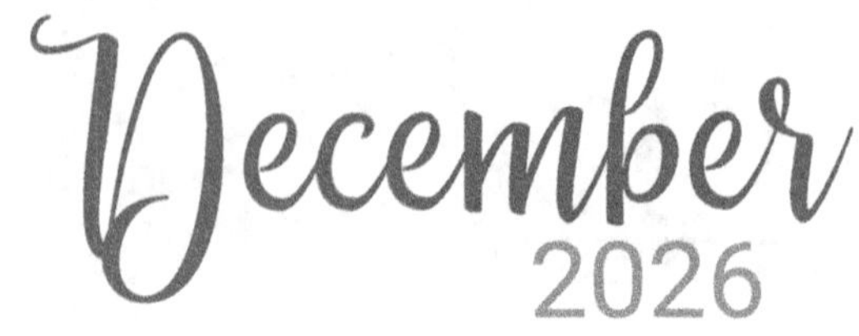



**05** SATURDAY

**06** SUNDAY

**07** MONDAY

**08** TUESDAY

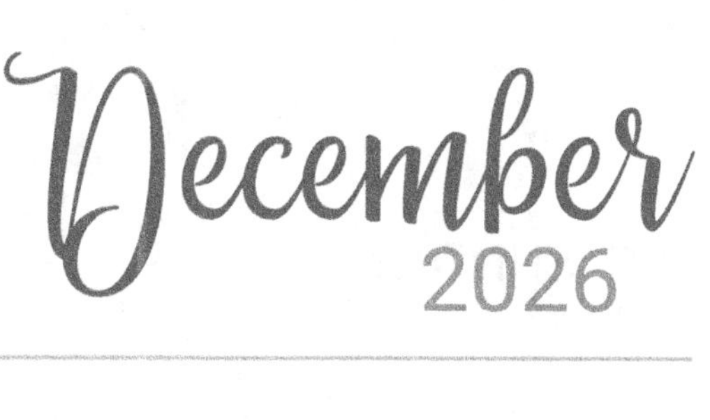

# December 2026

**09** WEDNESDAY

**10** THURSDAY

**11** FRIDAY

**12** SATURDAY

**13** SUNDAY

**14** MONDAY

**15** TUESDAY

**16** WEDNESDAY

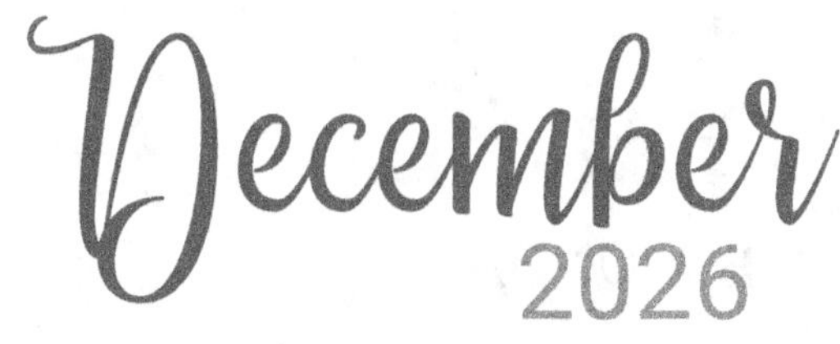


**17** THURSDAY

**18** FRIDAY

**19** SATURDAY

**20** SUNDAY

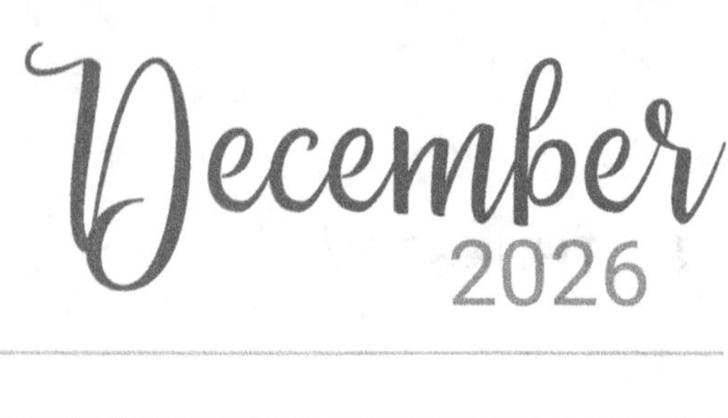

# December
## 2026

**21** MONDAY

**22** TUESDAY

**23** WEDNESDAY

**24** THURSDAY

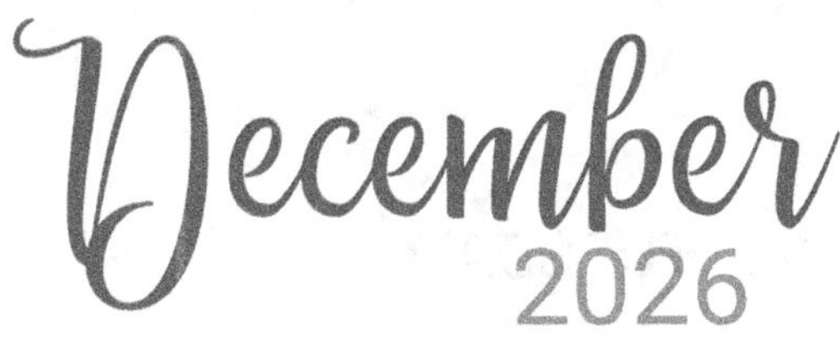


**25** FRIDAY

**26** SATURDAY

**27** SUNDAY

**28** MONDAY

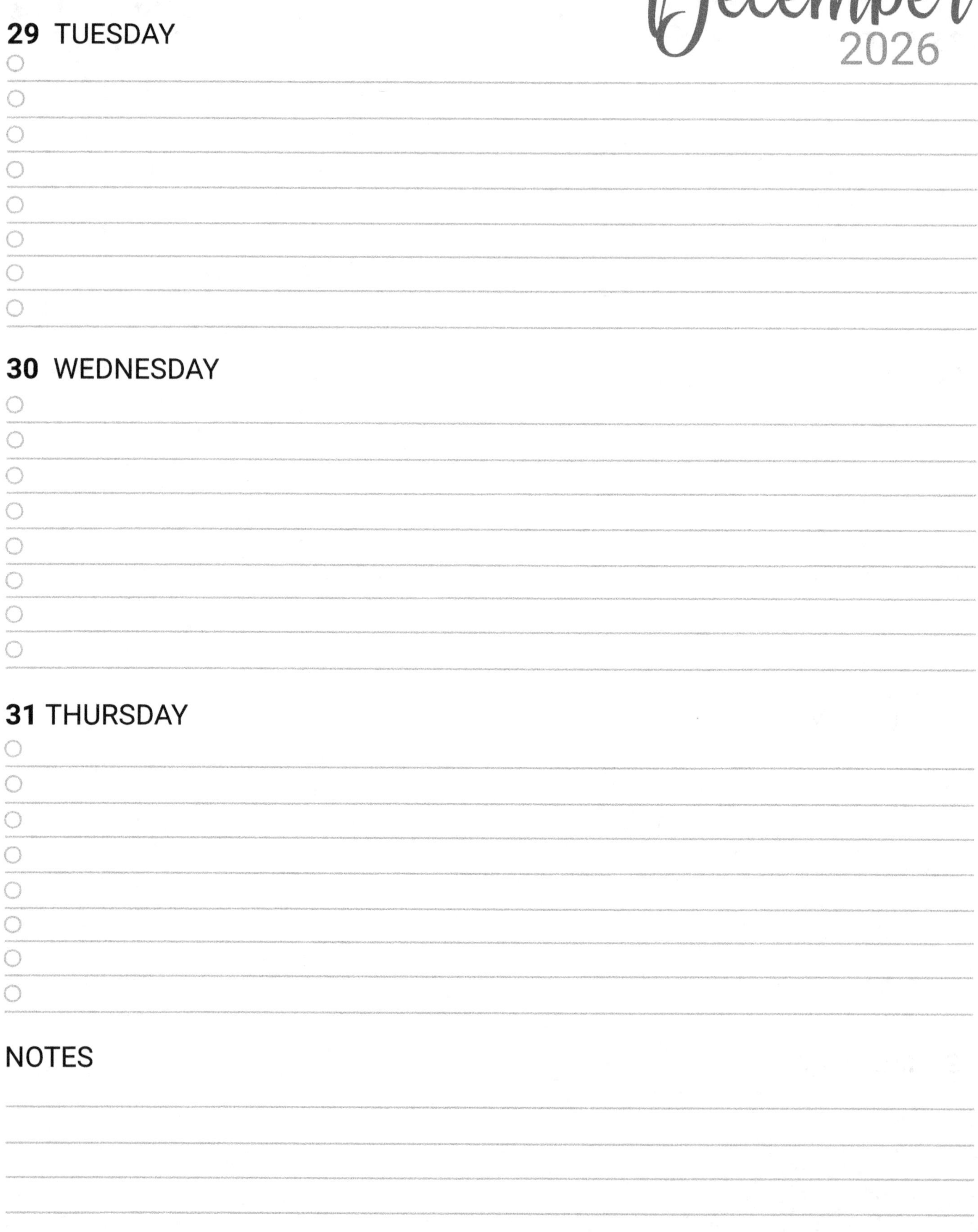



**29** TUESDAY

**30** WEDNESDAY

**31** THURSDAY

NOTES